W9-BLA-887

Fast Cash
With Quick-Turn
Real Estate

*How anyone can quickly
turn single family houses
into cash without using
money or credit.*

Ron LeGrand

"This publication is designed to provide accurate and authoritative information in regard to the subject matter covered. It is sold with the understanding that the publisher is not engaged in rendering legal, accounting, or other professional service. If legal or other expert assistance is required, the services of a competent professional person should be sought."

From a declaration of principles jointly adopted by a committee of the American Bar Association and a committee of the Publishers Association.

It is agreed that all controversies and claims between the reader or purchaser and the author and SDI LeGrand Publishing, Inc. will be settled by binding arbitration in Jacksonville, Florida in accordance with the Commercial Arbitration Rules of the American Arbitration Association ("AAA") or other arbitrators who are mutually agreeable to parties. Discovery will be governed by the Florida Rules of Civil Procedure, and the Attorneys of the record for the parties will be appointed umpires for the limited purpose of issuing subpoenas for discovery and for the arbitration hearing upon filing of a notice of appearance with the arbitrators. A copy of each subpoena will be filed with the arbitration in the public records. The arbitrators will award whomever prevails reasonable attorney's fees and costs, defined to include fees paid to arbitrators and expert witnesses. This agreement to arbitrate will be specifically enforceable under the prevailing arbitration law, and judgment upon the order rendered by the arbitrators may be entered by any court having jurisdiction thereof.

By retaining and reading this book, the reader or purchaser has agreed to be bound by the terms of the above paragraph regarding arbitration. If the purchaser, prior to reading the book, wishes to return the book, he or she may do so by mailing the book to SDI LeGrand Publishing, Inc. at the above address, or by calling customer service at 904-886-2985.

Copyright © 2001 SDI LeGrand Publishing, Inc.
All rights reserved. Except for reviews, no parts
of this book may be reproduced in any form
without the written permission of the publisher.

Printed in the United States of America 9 8 7 6 5 4 3 2 1 00
ISBN 0-9654851-0-2

Table of Contents

SECTION III - SMART MARKETING

SECTION IV - SAVVY DEALING

SECTION V - MONEY AND LAWS

SECTION VI - SUCCESS

ACKNOWLEDGMENTS

This book is the result of many years of learning in the school of hard knocks. Its principles have evolved out of my experience buying and selling houses, something I've done every day for 14 years. I wasn't born with this skill. I learned it. And you can learn it, too.

I have been successful in real estate because I took action and because I asked for help when I needed it. Equally important has been the support of people who are close to me. It is important to recognize their contributions to my success in the world of residential property investment.

First, I want to thank my wife, Beverly, for blessing me with a happy, 30-year marriage and for being at my side while I was learning to Quick-Turn houses. We've been through good and bad times together, and we agree the good times are better. But, our true wealth is our four children and eight grandchildren.

Many thanks also to my daughter Vicki, my son-in-law Bobby, and to every member of my great staff for their invaluable help during the making of this book.

I am grateful to Mark O. Haroldsen for being an important influence in my life. Not only have I learned a great deal from Mark personally, but over the years his company, The Financial Freedom Report, has provided the educational format to provide me with the constant stream of information and motivation that was crucial to my success. Thanks, Mark and company! Keep up the good work.

Mark's first book, *How to Wake Up the Financial Genius Inside You*, had a great impact on my early progress. That book has touched the lives of more than two million readers; its message is as fresh and relevant today as it was when it was written.

I also wish to thank Robert Allen for his contribution. One of his two-day seminars first opened my eyes to the world of real estate. That began the legacy I'm now passing on to those whose lives I touch.

Above all, I would like to acknowledge and dedicate this book to you, the reader, and your future success in real estate.

PREFACE

When I began to write this book, I planned to write an auto-biography to impress you with my brilliance and success over the past 14 years. Then it occurred to me you could care less about my accomplishments. You want to know IF and HOW this book will help you!

Bear in mind, I've organized the contents clearly and logically so you can quickly achieve a working knowledge of my Quick-Turn real estate business. These pages include all the practical information you need to benefit fast by using the techniques I teach.

If you like what you read, and you put my words into action, this book will be the beginning of your financially rewarding career in Quick-Turning houses.

Whether you are a beginning investor or a pro who has already bought and sold many properties, this book will provide valuable new information about making Fast Cash. Regardless of your level of expertise, you will learn new approaches to making money faster, safer, and easier than you ever dreamed possible. This information will also motivate you to continue to learn and grow by welcoming new ideas and taking action in your everyday life.

One of the hardest things for me to learn as an investor was that I did not have all the answers. (As a matter of fact, I still haven't even heard all the questions!) I continue to buy books and tapes, and I attend seminars regularly even though I have been in the business for 14 years and have turned more than 1,000 houses. But, we all need to learn constantly to be competitive.

Besides giving you new ideas, this book could cause old ideas to resurface and trigger actions that will enable you to reach goals you previously had thought impossible. Pursue your dreams with dogged determination. This is America, and nobody has to sit in the cheap seats. At the end of your life, you won't regret the things you did, but you will regret what you left undone. Life is too short. Don't grow old lamenting lost opportunities.

You control your life and almost everything that happens in it. You can choose how much fun you have, how much money you make, and how well you'll live when you retire. Riches and fulfillment are abundant for the people who have knowledge and use it wisely. I'll help you gain the knowledge you need, but you are the one who must choose to act on it. What will you choose? A few stale crumbs, or the whole tasty loaf?

Read this material, underline it, and use it. Take maximum advantage of my 14 years on the street honing the techniques I teach. Do what I ask you to do, and you will have the same kind of freedom and abundance in your life that I enjoy. Consistent, persistent action is the key to making this happen. I encourage you to stretch — to do things you haven't done before so you can have things you haven't had before.

Who's in control here? You should be. But if you aren't, I'm going to teach you to take control — of your life and of your destiny. There's no better time to begin than NOW!

Ron LeGrand

FOREWORD

**By Robert Allen, Best-Selling author of *Nothing Down,
Creating Wealth* and *The Challenge***

Everybody has a dream. For many people that dream is making a better life for themselves and their families. And there are as many different ways to make that happen as there are people trying. Some people work eighteen hour days at a mom-and-pop business, some fight their way up the corporate ladder, and others spend their meager paychecks on the weekly lottery. The approaches are drastically different, but the dream is exactly the same. They all want something better.

If you're working for somebody else, you know that reaching that goal is exceedingly hard. You may be able to scrape by, riding someone else's coat tails, but to really make it big, you have to make a leap of faith and do it on your own.

Fourteen years ago, a dirt-poor, bankrupt auto mechanic took that leap of faith. He borrowed four hundred fifty dollars from friends and family, hoping what sounded like an unbelievable promise was the answer to his dream.

That mechanic was Ron LeGrand. And the money that he borrowed all those years ago was to attend one of my seminars. This was the beginning of Ron's real estate education.

Within a few months, Ron owned over 70 properties. He was paper-rich. But soon he sat down to pay his monthly bills, and realized he didn't have the money in his account to cover them. It was a wake-up call for Ron. He realized he needed to develop a way to make cash quickly from real estate. This was the beginning of his Quick-Turn System.

Since that time, Ron has quick-turned over 1100 properties, each one adding to his personal knowledge, wealth, and the Quick-Turn System. Ron doesn't have to scrape anymore. He drives a Mercedes, owns a huge, beautiful home, and never worries about the monthly bills...he's a millionaire, not just on paper, but in real life.

Over the years, Ron has taught his System to thousands, with amazing success. And it's easy for me to see why. His frank style and direct approach appeal to folks who want straight talk on how to make it big.

Realizing his dream of making his life better, Ron's goal now is to help people all over the country do the same thing. And I'm sure he'll succeed. Not since my book *Nothing Down* has there been an educator who knows more about the subject of Quick-Turning houses than Ron LeGrand.

If you're looking for a way to make part-time income; if you want to start your own business; if you're finally ready to make it big, then you've picked up the right book. I encourage you to read on...financial independence is in your hands.

Bob

KEYS TO SUCCESS
in Quick-Turn Real Estate

Anyone, including **YOU**, can profit from Quick-Turning single-family houses in days. You don't need credit or partners, and you need little or none of your own money. But you do need the **KNOWLEDGE** contained on these pages . . . for knowledge, converted to action, is the **KEY TO SUCCESS!**

Section I
Winners All Around

*Do what others won't for five years,
and you can do what others can't
for the rest of your life.*

Anonymous

Chapter 1

Fast Cash in Days, Not Years

I started in the real estate investment business after attending a two-day seminar back in 1982. Luckily, everything I learned there worked. I quickly discovered that finding the bargains was not difficult, but making the offers — especially the low, low offers — takes a lot of guts.

When you're just starting out, fear is normal, but it shouldn't stop you. If you're not a little scared when you begin to buy houses, you must have nerves of steel. Making money in real estate is not difficult, but it does take persistence, knowledge and courage.

Not long after that seminar, I had 276 rental units. That may sound wonderful, but I sat down to pay the family utility bills one day and discovered there wasn't enough money to cover them, which led me to take a hard look at how I had been investing. I had become a paper millionaire quickly. It had been easy to accumulate equity, but I had no cash. And you can't eat equity or pay bills with it. That's when I started to look for cash flow. It was this chain of events that led me to develop the Quick-Turn method to generate cash.

A person can make $10,000 to $50,000 or more in this business with just one deal, even in a low-priced market. It doesn't take many deals like that each year to make a good living. People often believe that real estate investment is risky, but in reality, many nine-to-five jobs are even riskier. Talk to the thousands of people who have been recently laid off about their marvelous "job security!"

Most people work all their lives to get pensions equal to half the wages they were earning — wages that didn't cover their bills. But you are different. You have the opportunity to take the future into your own hands and build a cash flow that will continue whether you have a job or not.

The first step is to take care of today's financial needs, before you start building your empire. Once those needs are met, and you possess the ability to generate cash, there are countless ways to turn that cash into a consistent flow and provide for a secure retirement.

YOU DON'T HAVE TO WAIT

Some people think the only way to make money in real estate is to buy a property, sit on it for 20 or 30 years, contend with bad tenants, plugged toilets and negative cash flow, then sell for a profit. But that assumes there is something left of the house, and that inflation hasn't decreased the property's value. It also assumes that, during the holding period, the owners don't get so frustrated with property management that they just throw up their hands and quit. My experience has shown that happens to many people.

My intention is not to discourage the use of real estate as a retirement tool, or to indicate that people shouldn't hold property for the long term. In fact, I honestly believe that the greatest profits take time to develop. Huge fortunes have been amassed (some accidentally, it must be admitted) by people who have sat on property for a long time, then awakened one day to find the value increased by 10, 20, or even 100 times the purchase price.

But most people don't have the luxury of time, or the blind luck to make money while they sleep. In addition, most people are not properly equipped with knowledge and a clear-cut action plan before they start to buy properties.

I've seen many people who think that owning a few houses will make them rich enough in five years to retire and go fishing all day. More often, the opposite happens. The houses drag down the owners, who weren't properly trained to deal with the problems of real estate ownership. Those owners didn't have the knowledge you're getting from this book.... Knowledge that will keep you, the investor, in control.

A Road Map to Success

If your intentions are to buy real estate to generate more CASH, and if you want to have that cash now rather than years from now, listen up. There is a way to do just that. It involves "flipping houses fast," which I call "Quick-Turning."

During the past 14 years, I have bought and sold more than 1,000 houses for Fast Cash profit. Along the way, I developed a system that anyone who has the desire and willingness to learn can duplicate and make work for them, regardless of their financial condition. We are going to study all the aspects of this system, step-by-step, in the following chapters.

If you think you need a lot of money and good credit, or that you have to be a genius to make money in real estate, FORGET IT. It just isn't so! In this book, you'll learn how to convert houses to Fast Cash, no matter where in America you live and regardless of whether you are wealthy or flat broke. In fact, if you are broke, you may actually have an advantage because you have no choice but to learn before you leap. Those who have money tend to leap before they learn, then blame their failure on the system, the economy, their spouses, their mothers-in-law, and everyone else except themselves. In this, or any other business, you have to learn the fundamentals before leaping.

The three basic reasons to buy non-owner/occupied real estate are:

1. Quick cash profits
2. Monthly cash flow
3. Long-term growth

"But wait," you say. "What about tax shelter?" FORGET IT! Those days are gone. Many properties bought for tax shelters before the 1986 tax change are now owned by the Resolution Trust Corporation (RTC) or some other lending institution. This is especially true for the large properties such as apartment and commercial buildings which are being sold for a fraction of their former value. I feel sure we are going to see an escalating national debt and much larger savings and loan problems until the government returns incentives to investors in such properties.

It's wise to have properties in each cash-goal category. Use some deals to generate quick cash now. Those profits can then be used for investing — and for creating other deals to produce a steady monthly cash flow to cover your living expenses. Once you're sure your family's needs are being met, you can afford to invest in some "keepers" for long-term growth. You'll learn more about these strategies in the following chapters. But, for now, I'll assume that you want to know how to make Fast Cash.

Indeed, generating profits quickly through real estate is the primary emphasis of this book. The four key types of Quick-Turn transactions that generate cash will be discussed in detail.

REWARDS FOR ACTION

One thing is sure: People always need a place to live! Why not be in a business that will never lack customers? Why not work at something that produces paychecks in the thousands, whether you are involved part-time or full-time? How would you like to go where you want, when you want, stay as long as you want, and never worry about what's happening while you're away? And then there's the recognition you'll get for being a person who can find houses for people who never thought they could be homeowners.

Best of all, why not be in a business that's recession proof? You will learn how to make money with real estate in spite of the economy, interest rates, or the market situation. The only real difference between the "haves" and the "have-nots" is knowledge converted to action.

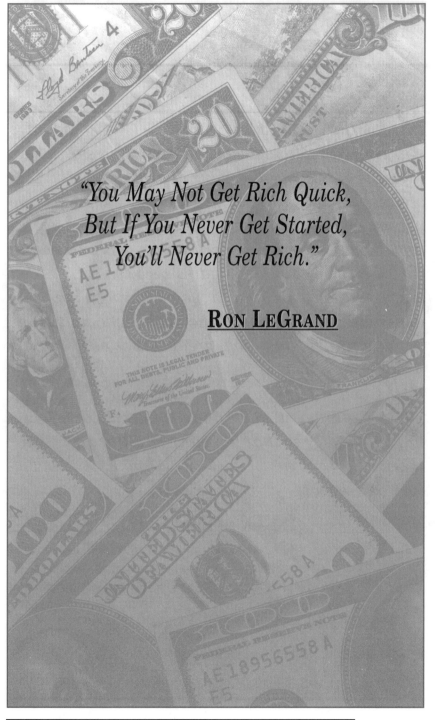

"*You May Not Get Rich Quick,
But If You Never Get Started,
You'll Never Get Rich.*"

RON LeGRAND

It's not the critic who counts: not the man who points out how the strong man stumbles or where the doer of deeds could have done them better. The credit belongs to the man who is actually in the arena, whose face is marred by dust and sweat and blood; who strives valiantly; who errs, and comes short again and again; because there is not effort without error and shortcoming; but who does actually strive to do the deals; who knows the great enthusiasms, the great devotions; spends himself on a worthy cause, who at the best knows in the end the triumphs of high achievement and who at the worst, if he fails, at least fails while daring greatly so that his place shall never be with those cold and timid souls who know neither victory nor defeat.

Theodore Roosevelt

Chapter **2**

Everyone Wins or I Won't Play

Some outsiders are under the impression that the only way to make money in Quick-Turn real estate is to take advantage of people. They picture all of us investors literally stealing houses and putting little old ladies out on the street. Or they perceive us as tyrannical landlords wearing big black hats and operating slum properties unfit for human habitation. Such perceptions are not just erroneous — they demonstrate total ignorance.

In all the years I have been an investor, buying more than 1,000 houses, not once have I ever put a gun to a seller's head and said, "Sign or die." In fact, many times I have found myself hoping the seller wouldn't work with me because I didn't like the looks of a deal. But, I went ahead and bought anyway, to get the seller out of a jam.

Many people don't understand the valuable services real estate entrepreneurs perform for the public. Of course, I wouldn't buy a house if I couldn't make a profit from it, but in many cases I could have walked away and been happier than if I was buying. However, the seller's needs pushed me to take on some project or other that may not have been the best use of my time.

NO FUN IN FORECLOSURE

In looking at the real estate business, several elements must be considered. It is more than money. Money is only the by-product of a specialized activity that provides one of life's necessities — shelter. Think about the last sad story you heard about a family home lost to foreclosure. Maybe you, yourself, have been through hard times and lost your house to a bank. How would you have felt about an investor providing you with a solution when no one else could or would? I can tell you from experience that there are few things in life more humiliating and stressful than lenders hounding you almost daily, demanding payments you can't cough up.

Going through that process destroys your self-esteem, breaks up marriages, and can even cause health problems — or worse. I once bought a house whose owner — the father of three children — had committed suicide under the stress of pending foreclosure. That experience gave me a new outlook on life. While I was buying the widow's house at 8 o'clock one Saturday night, trying to help her stop crying, I decided my measly little problems didn't amount to "a hill of beans" compared to hers.

She had three kids, but she had no income, no job, no food, and now no husband. All of a sudden I switched from the mindset of "How cheaply can I get this house?" to "How much can I afford to give this lady?" She owed about $26,000 on a $50,000 house; the monthly payment was $280. She was six months behind on her payments, and the house needed about $2,000 in repairs. She told me that if I would give her $1,000 and make up her payments, she would deed the house to me.

Now, I'm no angel, and I'm usually pretty reluctant to give up a buck unless it's absolutely necessary. But that night was an exception. I reached into my wallet and handed her $500 cash. Then I told her that, once I had checked her title and she was out of the house, I would give her an additional $3,500. That's $3,000 more than she was asking. Needless to say, she was elated, and I had won a friend for life.

But who really got the best of the bargain? Yes, I made money on the house. And I could have made $3,000 more. But the most important result of the deal was that I was on a high for weeks afterward, and I learned a lesson that will stick with me for life: You can't help someone up a hill without getting closer to the top yourself!

Remembering that experience still gives me goosebumps.

And I'm sure that, as your career progresses, you'll have more than one opportunity to help a similar family solve its problems.

Saving Houses From the Wrecking Ball

In addition to the human element, of course, there's also the matter of the houses themselves. Think of all the houses that are rehabbed by investors every week. If investors don't buy them, who will? What happens to them?

The answer is that they get bulldozed, or they just sit there until they are boarded up and condemned, then fall down of their own accord. True, every once in a while an owner/occupant buys a property to fix up and occupy. But for every one of those, 100 get rehabbed for profit by people like us. We are providing a service to our community by improving the looks of the neighborhood, as well as by increasing the stock of houses and the community's tax base. That, in turn, generates more revenue for the city.

In addition, the rehabbing requires contractors and laborers who benefit from the work. All rehabs require materials which are supplied by vendors who buy from manufacturers — all businesses which create jobs and employ people. And the process generates fees for professionals such as surveyors, REALTORS®, appraisers, termite inspectors, closing agents, title clerks, attorneys, etc. Stop the rehabbing of houses, and all those people suffer directly or indirectly. Many could not exist. So, yes, people who buy and fix houses certainly are performing a public service.

Sharing the Wealth

Let's look at aspects of real estate investing that have nothing to do with the rehabbing process itself. Have you ever known someone who has had to make two house payments simultaneously because he purchased a new home before the old one was sold? When I offer a lease/option deal, the seller usually accepts because he is seeking debt relief.

Who besides an investor is going to offer debt relief when a house doesn't sell? The REALTOR® maybe? Hardly. REALTORS® attempt to sell houses at little or no risk to themselves. Making a seller's payments while tying up a house for six months is not part of a REALTOR'S® service.

Could a seller rent the house to a tenant? Possibly! More often than not, all he or she would wind up with is an expensive lesson in landlording, and a bigger problem. Renting the house could also make it extremely difficult to sell. It would rarely be clean, and getting access to it would be complicated. Of course, the tenant would not be cooperating with the seller if it meant that, when the house was sold, the tenant would have to move.

So we investors step in and guarantee payments and repairs, and we usually get the house sold in time. The seller's problem is solved, and we have provided a public service. (Lease options are discussed in detail in Chapter 8.)

Believe it or not, while we're working to help sellers by saving them from the foreclosure machinery of the big bad banks, we're also performing a service for those banks. And that service, too, trickles down to a wider public. If investors didn't buy houses out of foreclosure or afterward, who would? If the only market was owner/occupants, you would see a drastic decline in housing prices. Moreover, the conditions for getting a loan would become terribly stringent. These factors would slow demand drastically, and all related industries would suffer. Many would evaporate.

There's still another very important group of people who benefit from investors' work in real estate. What about all those owner/occupants who wouldn't have a home of their own without us? I have sold hundreds of houses to first- and last-time home buyers. Many of them needed help solving minor problems and overcoming hurdles. I can honestly say some would never have been able to buy had I not made it possible.

Sometimes I helped them get financing. Sometimes I was the bank and owner-financed for them. Without my being the bank and allowing them to bypass rigorous qualifying procedures, most of those people would still be renters today. Usually, investors are the only owner-financing game in town.

Without us, owner financing would be almost nonexistent.

So are we providing a public service by understanding creative financing? You bet. We are providing a service that is extremely important to those families who could not own a home any other way. Incidentally, if it weren't for investors, who would own rental property, and where would all the tenants live?

True, as you become more and more involved with real estate investing, you may get the feeling that you're not always appreciated. Sometimes we catch a lot of flack from government employees, REALTORS®, and other people who don't understand the business. But rest assured, investors will be around as long as people need places to live. There is plenty of business to go around, and investors can make money without making anyone suffer. If any deal is not win/win, just don't do it.

Move on.

Section II
Quick-Turn Tools

The secret of success is constancy of purpose.

Benjamin Disraeli

Chapter

Four High-Voltage Cash Generators

Quick-Turn transactions fall into four main categories. Almost everything you do in the house business will follow one of these methods.

RETAILING

Buying houses low and selling them high is called retailing. This is the most easily understood method because there are countless books and tapes on the subject. It is the art of buying at a low price, often doing some repairs, then selling at retail price, usually cashing out. There is a lot of money in this method. Some people do this part-time, turning only two or three houses a year, and make more money at it than they make on their regular jobs. We'll discuss the buy low-sell high method in Chapter 5.

WHOLESALING

The second method is wholesaling. This is an entire business in itself and generates super-fast profits, usually without ever requiring the title to a property. It's not uncommon to pick up a check at closing, with the seller and buyer present at the same time. Many times I have earned thousands of dollars within two or three days of finding a deal. Successful people in the wholesale business are accomplished at locating good deals and marketing them — primarily to people who are in the buy low-sell high business. The first purchaser is willing to take a smaller, fast profit and leave the larger profit to an investor who has the time and money to buy, repair, and sit on the house until it is sold.

Some of my students are making a good income by buying, then reselling immediately, only once or twice a month. These deals require no money, no credit, no partners, and no bosses. Believe me, if you locate the deal, there is someone waiting to buy it from you. We'll cover all that in detail in Chapter 6.

ASSUMPTIONS

The third method involves assumptions. Millions of Americans would love to own a home but, for a variety of reasons, either don't qualify for a loan or don't want to borrow from a traditional lender -- even though they do have money for a down payment. With the assumption method, your job is to find good houses with existing no-qualifying loans. Or you can create opportunities through seller financing.

Thousands of existing FHA and VA loans may be assumed by anyone regardless of their credit. The idea is to find houses you can buy with little or no money, and flip them for a few thousand dollars more than you paid for them. Many owners will walk away with virtually nothing just to get the loan out of their names. Because the properties have assumable, no-qualifying loans, they're worth a little more and are easier to turn quickly.

All a purchaser needs to qualify is the down payment you are requesting. This kind of transaction usually takes only a few days to consummate and you don't have to stay in the junk house market to do it. In Chapter 7, you'll learn to manage assumptions with no credit, no partners, and very little training. And, you'll be working in first-class neighborhoods dealing in houses needing no repairs.

LEASE/OPTIONS

The fourth method is to lease/option properties to control them without taking title. This method works on houses in any condition, in any price range, and with any underlying financing. You can reap big profits without ever owning the house, while paying no closing costs to buy or sell, doing no repairs, and using very little or no money. In Chapter 8, you'll learn how to lease/option without even making monthly payments.

TAKING ACTION TO GET STARTED

You may be thinking all this is great, but I'm sure you're wondering where and how a person like you might get the money, find the bargains, and then get the houses sold. Relax! All of your questions will be answered in this book, and all your excuses for not taking action will be eliminated. When I began, I was bankrupt and broke, and I had absolutely no previous experience. That was about 1,000 houses ago. When I remember how little I knew when I started, then look at how far I've come, few, if any, excuses make sense.

Some of my students do 50 to 60 deals a year with an average net profit of $15,000 each. Remember, every one of those investors began just where you are today. By the time you finish this book, you will realize all you have to do is find the good deals. If you can find the deals, the money is easy to obtain. In fact, it's easy to obtain everything you need to get started in real estate investing.

The best place to begin, however, is with education. Just reading this book shows you're on the right track. Ignorance costs dearly. Many of the best deals in your real estate career will come from sellers who refuse to read a single book on the subject. They will end up selling their properties for tens of thousands of dollars below value.

Don't stop with this book! You should constantly be learning, attending seminars, reading other books on the subject, and using what you learn to polish your real estate investing techniques. My friend James A. Ray once told me an interesting story. When he was starting in the business, he met someone who had bought a real estate seminar package, but had never listened to it. James bought it from the man for a small price and took it home that evening.

He listened to all the tapes in one sitting, studying the booklets that came with them until 4 a.m.! The next day he started to apply the principles he had learned, and bought his first investment house for $8,000. After some minor repairs, he lease/optioned the house to a couple for $30,000 at $500 a month. Ever since then, he has been investing in real estate full-time.

He now has a personal collection of about 80 seminar packages. His reason: he feels that he either saves or makes money every time he studies one. What would have happened had he chosen NOT to buy that first course?

As this story illustrates, just reading books and attending seminars is not enough. Like James, you must take action! Get out there and try. Put the principles you learn from this book into immediate practice. It is action that will separate you from the nine-to-five workaday crowd — the same people who will eventually retire on 50% of what they can't live on today!

You must focus on the word "now". You want cash **now** or cash flow **now**, using the four Quick-Turn methods: retailing, wholesaling, assumptions, and lease/options. But, to turn your dreams into reality, you must **TAKE ACTION!** Action determines whether you realize your goals or not. You can do a little and get a little, or you can do a lot and get a lot, but nothing will ever happen for you until you act.

Taking action can be making a phone call to a FSBO (For Sale By Owner - pronounced *"fizz bow"*), or it can be getting a REALTOR® to locate 20 houses that fit your investment parameters. A little action taken every day will grow to a big benefit in time. A lot of consistent action will yield a lot of benefits in a short time. I didn't invent these laws, but I have much more wealth in abundance because I follow them. Take action, ask, go, do, and your life will take a serious turn for the better.

*This reminds me of a letter from a student who chose to convert my home study course into action. His name is Dave Doucette, and he is from Long Mont, Colorado. I spoke for the **Financial Freedom Report** in Las Vegas in September 1991. Dave's wife saw me there and became excited about what she heard. Dave did not attend with her, as they tell the story. But after hearing me, she called him to say she was buying my course for him. He told her that if she felt that strongly about it, buying the course was OK. At least that's his side of the story. I haven't confirmed with her whether he put up a fight or not. Anyway, she took the material home, and he began to study it.*

I had no idea Dave and his wife even existed until I received a letter from them some months later. In the letter, they explained how they had used my course to net more than $100,000 in just nine months by Quick-Turning a few houses. Needless to say, that letter was the highlight of my day. But the story gets better. I met Dave and his wife in Las Vegas when I spoke there again, a year later. That's when they announced that the $100,000 profit mentioned in the letter had risen to $175,000 in 11 months!

Yes, I'm extremely proud of the Doucettes, and not because of the large amount of money they made. But they were among the fortunate minority of people who possess the ability to seek knowledge so they can recognize opportunity. Dave and his wife converted opportunity to action and took control of their own financial future. Bravo to the Doucettes!

Yet another example of taking action is illustrated by Phil Barnes of Toledo, Ohio. Phil said, "I recently bought and sold a home that I saw For Sale By Owner while we were on your boot camp bus. The owner was a truck driver and hard to find. The house had an assumable, non-qualifying loan with a $27,600 balance. After putting $3,500 into repairs, I

*sold it for $47,900, making a net profit of $16,800. I
want to say how much I appreciate the boot camp and
the information you gave us. As a result, my wife and
I are looking for bigger and better things to happen in
the future."*

Are you ready? Ready not just to read, but to DO something
about what you read? GOOD! Let's begin by examining what
constitutes a good investment.

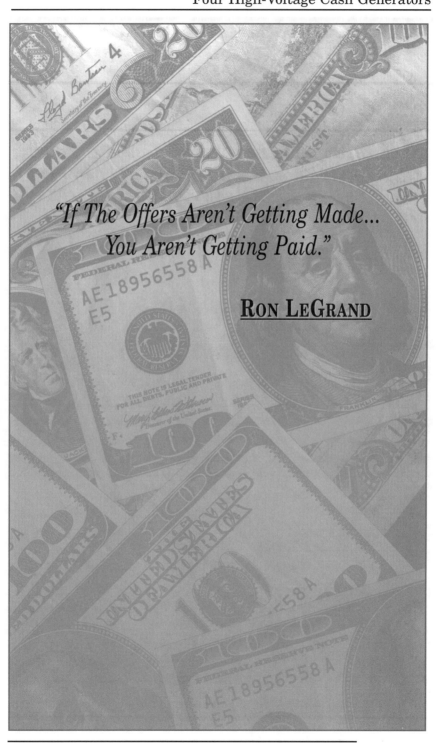

"*If The Offers Aren't Getting Made...
You Aren't Getting Paid.*"

RON LEGRAND

Success seems to be connected with ACTION. Successful men keep moving. They make mistakes, but they don't quit.

Conrad Hilton

Chapter **4**

Good Deals
Without Guessing

What is a good deal? It all depends on your objectives. A good deal is making the money you want in the time you allot. For some people that's a few days; for others it may be a few hours, a few weeks, or a couple of months. Some investors who are in the rental business believe it should take years to make a profit. I don't believe that and soon you won't either.

Let's illustrate with a real-life example. I once received a call regarding a flyer we had distributed. The voice on the other end said, "Hey, this flyer I'm holding says you buy houses. Is that true?"

"Yes, I sure do," I replied.

He said he had a house for sale. He wanted all cash, and he wanted to close that day. He told me that his mother had died and left him the house with clear title. He wanted to close fast and leave town. I asked him where the house was and how much he wanted.

When he told me the location and that he was asking only $12,000, I immediately knew that this was a great deal. Houses in that area were worth between $35,000 and $45,000 in good shape.

I told him I was interested and made an appointment to meet him there in a few minutes. Notice, I said minutes, not hours or days. When you smell a good deal, you'd better move FAST! You can't wait until it's convenient. If you don't move, someone else will. You can't Quick-Turn in slow motion.

I quickly met him at the house. His mother had lived there. She had four cats, and judging from the smell of the place, they had never gone outside. Other than that, I figured the house just needed some cosmetics and about $3,000 to get it into shape to sell. I ran through the house, saw what I wanted, and moved to the front yard to do our talking.

"Look man," I said, "you want me to close today, pay cash, clean up this mess, and get the stink out of the house. That's asking a lot. You've got to cut me some slack here!"

"If you can close today, I'll take $11,000, no less," he countered.

"Sign here" was my response.

I took his contract to the title company and told them to put a rush on it because I needed to close that afternoon. Sure enough, he had good title, and I bought the house that day. I used three credit cards for the purchase and spent an additional $3,200 for repairs.

I sold the property immediately for $39,000. All cash! It took exactly two months to the day to close the sale because the buyer got new financing, and at that time I didn't know how to take control of my buyer's new loan process. Today, it would take only 30 days.

My net profit on that one little house was about $23,000. Not bad, huh? By the way, I discovered that the flyer he had referenced was a year and a half old! We'll talk about flyers more in "Finding Motivated Sellers" in Chapter 9.

FOUR SIMPLE ACTIONS

To stay focused, I concentrate on my objectives. I constantly review in my mind how to find, buy, and sell single-family houses for cash. That's how I came up with my simple philosophy: **Find 'em, Fix 'em, Flip 'em, Forget 'em.**

CALCULATING PROFITABILITY

You should know, not guess, your net profit on a deal before you make an offer, not after you buy and repair the house! One of the most useful tools I have created is the Property Acquisition Worksheet, which is in Appendix A. Look that form over carefully. It will save you thousands of dollars by illustrating whether the property you are thinking of buying will fit your objectives.

This worksheet is the one I take along when looking at a property. After 14 years and 1,000 houses, I still use this form to lay out all the numbers I need to determine whether a given house will make money or not. The worksheet is the result of taking these steps repeatedly and becoming very successful at it. If you want to reinvent the wheel, feel free; if you want to make money quickly, learn to use this simple document. It will keep you from being shocked when you see the real bottom line.

For example, I found a house with a purchase price of $20,000. The property was in serious disrepair. That's why it was so cheap. It's estimated sale price was $44,500 after repairs. It had an existing first mortgage of $5,000. I gave the seller $5,000 down, and he took back a second mortgage for $10,000, all due and payable in six months, with no payments and no interest, because I knew he would be paid off within that time frame.

My total cost as calculated on the worksheet showed that it would take $10,000 to develop this deal. I paid $20,000 for the house (including the first mortgage balance) and spent $10,000 for fix-ups and other costs. I had $30,000 in it and sold it for a retail price of $44,000, which left me with a net profit of $14,000. At first glance, it had looked as though my profit would be $16,000 to $18,000, but the true amount was revealed when all the hidden costs were considered. Use this worksheet without exception to save yourself a lot of grief.

SELLING TO ANOTHER INVESTOR

The Property Acquisition Worksheet (Appendix A) will also show an investor looking for a wholesale deal how much he can expect to make if he purchases the contract. Just by looking at the completed form, especially the bottom line, he can decide if he wants to buy the property. All the numbers are on the sheet. Remember, it should be filled out before you decide to buy. In fact, you should complete it before you make an offer.

EXPLANATION OF THE PROPERTY
ACQUISITION WORKSHEET

- Use comparables, appraisals, or your knowledge of the neighborhood to determine the sale price of property before you ever make an offer. Never buy a property until you know this value after fix-up. If you neglect to be careful about this, you're headed for an expensive lesson in the real world.

- **Items 2-9** relate to the purchase cost. Include every applicable item. The down payment is what you will pay the seller at closing. Closing costs vary depending on the type of financing. Talk to your REALTOR® or a lending officer to determine exact figures for your deal.

  The appraisal may be an FHA, VA, or fee appraisal. It depends on financing obtained and may cost between $250 and $400. The termite inspection is paid by either the seller or the buyer. Prices vary from $20 to $75 depending on the size of the property and type of inspection. The survey is performed by a licensed engineer; fees start at about $250. Miscellaneous costs include bird dog fees and fees for putting utilities in your name, to name a few.

- **Items 10-12** deal with repair costs. You can get formal written estimates from contractors. If it's set up so that the contractor will be responsible for all the repairs, and if you have the estimate in writing, it will be the contractor's problem if the actual cost exceeds the estimate. Nevertheless, allow for cost overruns from hidden problems.

  Sometimes, I use several contractors for the same job, such as a roofer, a plumber, and an A/C contractor. This requires several estimates. In the beginning, I suggest that you get multiple bids on every deal, but only after you have the property under contract. Don't waste time collecting information on properties you're not buying. See if you have a deal, then spend time on the house. Soon, you'll be able to estimate costs without getting bids. You'll learn to make an offer based on your immediate assumptions and verify those assumptions before closing. You'll be able to buy while others are still collecting information.

- **Items 13-17** show you what it will cost to hold the property in terms of monthly payments and other expenses. Allow for at least six months' worth of expenses if you're selling retail. The "payments for six months" item refers to the mortgage payment, if any, during the fix-up and sale period. The property tax amount can be found by contacting a title company, an attorney, or a county clerk. In Quick-Turning houses, you will seldom pay any property tax except at closing. Insurance is in reference to a basic hazard insurance policy on the property for the time you own it. Similarly, the figure for utilities refers to the electricity, gas, and water used while the house is in your name.

- **Items 18-21** show you what it will cost to sell the property. This is the cost of actually closing the loan and executing the sale. If you need help estimating these costs, simply call the lender you want to use and give him the sale price. He will prepare a cost estimate for you and tell you what the seller must pay. Remember to use only those costs you are paying, not the total sale costs. Some costs will be covered by the buyer.

Next add lines 9, 12, 17, and 21 and subtract the total from the amount for which you expect to sell the property. Then subtract existing mortgages you have to pay off. This gives you your net profit.

Finally, to determine exactly how much cash it will take to buy this property — the bottom line — add items 9, 12, 13, 15, 16, and 20. These are items that require a cash outlay during the holding period. The other items will be deducted at closing.

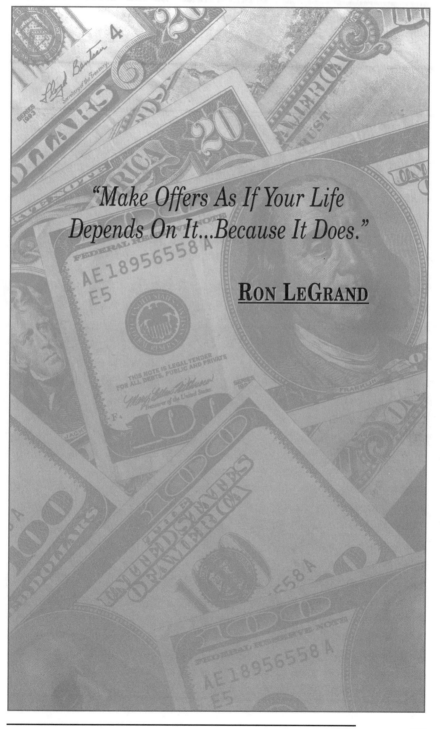

"*Make Offers As If Your Life Depends On It...Because It Does.*"

RON LEGRAND

The dictionary is the only place
where success comes before work.

Arthur Brisbane

Chapter **5**

Retailing to Owner/Occupants

BUY LOW-SELL HIGH

As noted in the previous chapter, there are really only four ways to turn Fast Cash profits with houses: retailing, wholesaling, assumptions, and lease options. Almost any kind of Quick-Turn transaction you create will fall into one of these categories.

One of the most widely accepted methods for making quick profits with single-family houses is to buy low — well below the after-repaired value — then rehab the property to market to an owner/occupant at retail price via new financing. This retailing method I call "buy low-sell high." This kind of deal is concerned with price, whether it involves an all-cash deal, very little cash down, or no cash at all. Most important is your net — the amount you keep after expenses. This is the type of deal that brings in the most money, but it also has the most headaches.

In Chapter 15, I show you how to market these houses quickly. During the past 14 years, I have bought and sold at least 100 houses using the buy low-sell high method alone. You can earn huge profits in a short time by flipping houses. By "short time" I mean 2 to 6 months, on average. An example of this is a house I bought for $22,000 by putting down $5,000 of a partner's money and taking over existing loans. We spent $5,000 of my partner's money to repair the house, which we sold in 30 days for $49,000 with a new FHA loan for the buyer. This whole transaction took 60 days from the time we purchased the house to the time we closed the sale. However, this is not always the case. Sometimes you hold properties for several months. Don't let an extended holding period put you in a difficult spot. Plan for it going in. Then, if you can sell the house quickly, you get an added bonus.

A UNIVERSAL MECHANISM

I know you folks in the higher-priced markets are laughing at these figures, but believe me, if prices are much higher in your area, you have a definite advantage. In an area like Los Angeles where the houses start at $100,000, it's much easier to make a lot more money with fewer deals.

On my little house, we netted about a 40% profit. However, I don't want to lead you to believe that you should expect a 40% profit in high-dollar markets. The percent of profit is not important; all that counts is the dollars. Would you rather have 40% of my $49,000, or 20% of $175,000? Tough decision, huh?

> *At one of my recent Los Angeles classes, a student told me how he had made a $50,000 profit on his first investment house, mostly by accident. He had simply bought an inexpensive house and done some work on it so his son could live in it. But when he discovered that the house was worth about $60,000 more than he had paid for it four months earlier, they decided to sell it. It wasn't inflation that increased the value and allowed that kind of profit. It was sweat equity and a smart decision to buy a property well below market price. Their profit was made when they purchased and realized when they sold.*

Sometimes, I wish I had cut my teeth on high-dollar houses. I often wonder how much more money I might have made during the past 14 years had I been dealing in houses costing more than $100,000 rather than less.

A couple of students from the Washington, D.C. area come to mind. Their names are Keith and Kyong Luck.

I remember that the first deal we discussed was a foreclosure in which they were involved. The house was worth about $220,000 and in good condition. The Lucks had gone through a series of negotiations with the seller and the seller's attorney, only to have the attorney blow the whole deal. The Lucks were willing to pay $150,000 to $160,000 for the house with some owner financing, but the attorney had advised the sellers they could do better, and that a miracle would happen before they were foreclosed out of the house.

Finally, the foreclosure auction was looming, and no miracle had occurred, so the Lucks stopped talking to the seller and the attorney and went directly to the lender, the one who was foreclosing. With him, they negotiated a deal in which the bank would create a new loan to the Lucks for the amount of the existing debt if the sale went through and the bank got the house back. Of course, no miracle happened, the sale went through, and the sellers lost their house because they had followed the advice of their brilliant counsel.

All this time, Kyong had been telling me she wanted to buy a house for 50 cents on the dollar. I kept telling her that doing so would be difficult in her high-dollar market. I bet I told her a half dozen times that 20% of $200,000 was better than 50% of my $50,000 houses. I finally got her to agree to stop trying to make a killing on one house and to be happy with a 20% to 30% profit in her area. So she agreed to be less greedy and to stop making ridiculous offers.

Their next call was to tell me they had bought the house from the bank the day after the sale. The bank issued them a new $95,000 loan with good terms, and they had to agree to throw an additional $6,000 into the pot to get the house. Their total purchase price was $101,000 for a $220,000 house in good condition.

I'll tell you, some of my students just won't listen. Maybe the next time I tell them they can't buy a house for half price they'll pay attention. Then again, maybe not. By the way, after the Lucks bought this house they did a stupid thing. They moved into it. Dumb, huh? The last time I heard, they had refinanced the house for $175,000 to generate about $70,000 of tax-free cash. Knowing Kyong, I'll bet she still has every penny of it.

Any of you, and I do mean any of you, who have a desire to use real estate as your vehicle, coupled with willingness to learn what you need to make it work, can accomplish the same thing and more. If you put forth the effort and stick with it long enough, you will be successful. Most folks start part-time and learn the ropes as they go. After a few successes, some make it their full-time occupation. After all, if you net $10,000 or more per house, how many do you have to turn in a year to surpass your present income?

SALEABLE HOUSES FOR PENNIES ON THE DOLLAR

The kind of "buy low-sell high" house you're looking for is located in a bread-and-butter neighborhood, the subdivisions that are in the low to mid range-priced houses. This is where most Americans live. This is where you will find the majority of the houses with the most motivated sellers, and that is where most buyers want to live.

If you intend to sell using FHA financing, ascertain the maximum loan for your area and look for houses that will retail in a range from 40% to 65% of that amount. For example, if $90,000 is the maximum loan, then you will look for houses that will appraise for $35,000 to $60,000 in good condition. If you venture above that range, you will have a tough sale on your hands because your buyers will need a large down payment to qualify for financing.

You'll spend much more time trying to market a high priced house than you will if you stick to the low-priced bread-and-butter houses. Why tie up your funds in one really nice house when you could take the same money and get control of three or four houses in blue-collar neighborhoods? The people who buy higher-priced houses are more sensitive to ripples, bangs, and thuds in the economy than the blue-collar guys.

Think about it. When the vice president of marketing is laid off, how long will it take him to find a comparable position? When the guy who works at the plant or works construction gets laid off, he can usually find a similar job in a lot less time than will the vice president. Another thing to consider is that many houses in the upper end of the market require two incomes to make the mortgage payment. What happens if one spouse gets laid off, pregnant, or dies?

Give this serious thought when you are prospecting for properties. In other words, do your fishing in the pond with the most fish. You need to do everything possible to ensure the success of your investments.

Next, find out how much the property is going to cost. Using the Property Acquisition Worksheet will help you calculate this in a matter of minutes, and it will keep you from forgetting anything. After you have completed the worksheet, the only thing left is to verify your assumptions, which are the cost of repairs and the value after the repairs are made. If the numbers tell you you'll make the desired profit, and the house is in a saleable neighborhood, then proceed to closing.

Summarizing, here are the essentials for a buy low-sell high deal:

1. You must make sure the house is in a good location for resale — a good, clean neighborhood where people want to live and where you won't need a gun to feel safe while showing the house.

2. Complete the Property Acquisition Worksheet. Make sure you know your bottom line prior to buying the property. Know what you are going to do with the property. The worksheet will show you the profit you can expect if you enter into a particular deal.

3. Perform quality repairs to the house. Don't cheat in this area because you're in a hurry to resell. If you have a

buyer who can qualify for a loan, he or she has many houses from which to choose. Your house should be prepared so that it is a cut above the rest.

4. Prepare a complete marketing plan for the house before you put it up for sale. Answer these questions before you buy the house: How are you going to sell it? Who is going to sell it? What lender are you going to use? How will you write the ad? The earlier you decide these matters, the smoother the sale will go and the faster you will make your cash profits.

It may be to your advantage to let a good REALTOR® handle the sale for you if you don't feel comfortable doing it yourself. If you have done a good job of finding a good deal to begin with, you should be able to afford the services of a REALTOR® and still make a handsome profit for yourself. Remember, no one gets anything until the property is sold. Professionals can sometimes help you turn the houses faster than you can do it yourself. Used properly, a REALTOR® can be a real asset in your investment strategy. In later chapters, we'll talk more about REALTORS® and how they can put more cash in your pocket.

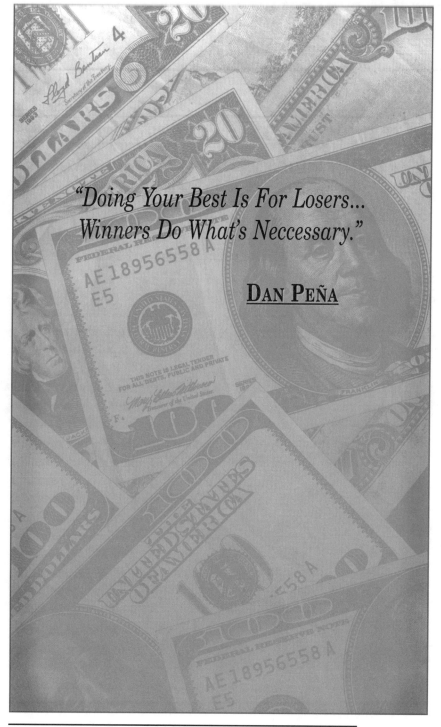

"*Doing Your Best Is For Losers...*
Winners Do What's Neccessary."

DAN PEÑA

Obstacles are those frightful things you see
when you take your eyes off your goals.
A great pleasure in life is doing
what people say you cannot do.

Walter Gagehot

Chapter 6

Wholesaling to Other Vendors

BUY LOW-SELL LOW

Wholesaling properties is one of the best methods to generate rapid returns. As we said in the previous chapter, although retailing a property will make more money, it requires far more work. To retail, you need money to purchase and repair; you must find a buyer; and you have to arrange a loan. If you are willing to do that much work, retailing is the way to make the most money.

It is wise, however, not to have too many retail houses going at any one time. It is too hard and risky because of carrying costs. On the other hand, just because you have plenty of houses to retail, you shouldn't stop looking for more because wholesale buyers are always available if you find a good deal.

Wholesaling properties is the quickest way to make cash overnight. For example, I recently bought a house from a lender for $5,000 total. The house needed work and was appraised for $32,000 after repairs. I sold it the next day for $10,000 cash without touching it. The lender could just as well have spent $5,000 to fix it up and sold it retail for $32,000. He didn't want to do this, for various reasons, so his loss was my gain.

The hardest part about wholesaling is finding the deals. You will learn how to do that in Chapter 9. When you become good at finding the deals, you are often a retailer's best source for houses. You, as a wholesaler, can look for deals all day, all the time. You may have to make 20 offers to get one that is acceptable to a wholesale buyer. However, if you are willing to do the hard work, it is not uncommon to make $2,000 to $10,000 in 24 to 48 hours with a good contract. A person can make a good living finding deals to sell to investors and/or owner occupants, without ever retailing a single house.

With this method, you find the properties, put them under contract, then sell the contract to other investors who want to make repairs and sell properties retail. In some cases, you will have to purchase the house to protect the deal and sell it a short time later for a quick profit. Usually, a retailer is our prime customer, but owner occupants are good candidates as well, because many people are looking for inexpensive handyman specials they can fix up and occupy.

SELLING A CONTRACT TO ANOTHER INVESTOR

Four keys to wholesaling your properties:

1. **Don't expect to sell an investor any house you wouldn't buy for yourself.** You have to negotiate good deals if you are going to get into the wholesale business. Remember, investors aren't stupid; they think just like you.

   Ask yourself if you would buy the contract in question if it were presented to you and you had the money, but not enough time to find your own deals. Remember, if buyers are going to do all the work to repair a property and market it at retail, they want to make a good profit, and they are entitled to it.

2. **Complete the Property Acquisition Worksheet,** without exception. Fill out this sheet as if you were the investor who was going to buy the house and retail it. Allow for a reasonable profit for the investor, while making sure that you include your own wholesale profit in your buyer's costs.

3. **Don't be greedy!** Take a small, fast profit, leaving the larger profit to the retailer. You can sell the contract to an investor for a markup of $2,000 to $10,000, letting the investor repair the house and collect the lion's share of profits.

Remember, there is always a wholesale market and a retail market. It is the wholesale market that lets you turn a deal into quick profits. You should be willing to take less money to complete the deal more quickly. Using this method, you will ultimately make more money by working a larger number of deals, each generating a modest profit.

The amount of your profit will depend upon the value of each deal, your quickness at finding the great bargains, and your skill at cultivating a list of wholesale buyers who will buy the houses as fast as you can find them.

4. **Construct these deals with low cash down.** For example, in the deal mentioned below, we could have offered the seller $15,000 cash to mortgage, taken over the $5,000 loan, and bought this $20,000 house. But if we had done that, the investor would have had to come up with $17,000 cash to buy this property from us. That would have been too high for some investors.

Constructing the deal with only $7,000 cash down made it much more marketable. Make your deal acceptable to the seller and agreeable to an investor, so you can turn it around with as little cash as possible. Make your deals work for everybody!

EXAMPLE

OFFER 1

Purchase Price	$ 20,000
Take existing debt	$ 5,000
Cash required	$ 15,000
Plus my fee	$ 2,000

TOTAL CASH REQUIRED $ 17,000

OFFER 2

Purchase Price	$ 20,000
Take existing debt	$ 5,000
Down to seller	$ 5,000
Short term seller carry back	$ 10,000
Cash required	$ 5,000
Plus my fee	$ 2,000

TOTAL CASH REQUIRED $ 7,000

Always be cash-conscious. Make offers as if you have little or no money, even if you have a lot. The smaller amount of cash required, the more attractive the deal will be to an investor. And, of course, always use as much seller financing as possible.

FINDING OTHER INVESTORS TO BUY FROM YOU

A great place to find buyers for your contracts is your local real estate club. Some clubs in major metropolitan areas have several hundred investors, many of whom are potential buyers for your contracts.

Why would they want to buy your contracts? Many investors don't have the time to find as many deals as they would like. Some investors are too busy to even follow up on their own leads! Others may be nervous about negotiating and will be thankful for the opportunity to profit from your initiative. Occasionally, investors will have chosen a narrow niche in the market in which they want to work, such as a particular neighborhood or type of building. If you bring in their kind of contract, they will be extremely interested.

To find a club, just check the yellow pages under "clubs" or "associations." Sometimes clubs advertise in newspapers. Be sure to ask REALTORS®, title insurance companies, real estate attorneys, and others who work in the field if they know of any local real estate clubs. If there isn't a club, start one! You will quickly discover just how many other investors that do or want to do the same thing you do. Real estate associations are discussed further in Chapter 9.

In addition to real estate clubs, you can run ads in the local papers. People who call about handyman specials are usually investors. Keep those names and treasure them because they are your most valuable assets. Be sure to complete an information sheet for each investor. Before long, you will have developed a list of serious buyers, and then your problem will be finding deals fast enough to sell to them.

The Property Acquisition Worksheet is one of the best tools in your investor tool kit. First, it will tell you whether the deal makes sense or not. When I say a deal "makes sense," I mean that a property can be bought for a price low enough to cover all costs, then sold high enough to render a profit. Whether I sell a house to an investor or to a home buyer, I have to be able to meet the costs AND realize enough profit to make the deal worthwhile.

When an investor sees that you have taken into account all the costs involved in a piece of property, while allowing a profit margin for both of you, he feels the deal is attractive and you are a pro. Remember, this is not about real estate; it is about money. If your investors don't want to buy or can't buy at the moment, ask them if they know anyone else who might be interested in buying a house for renovation and resale. Even a person who can't afford the deal may know someone who can.

If you are able to find good deals, you won't have trouble selling them. Only time will make you an expert at wholesaling. Don't expect to acquire all the answers in a day.

One mistake many investors make is to stop looking for houses when they have a few on hand. When you become proficient at finding the bargains, you will probably discover that they are much easier to find and buy than they are to sell retail to qualified buyers. However, this should not stop you from wholesaling them as fast as you can find them.

Most of the time, you will have a house sold before you have to buy it. By constantly locating deals for others, a high, consistent cash flow may be obtained by collecting a few thousand dollars per house on simple, hassle-free Quick-Turns. Many of my students are producing $15,000 or more in monthly income by doing just that. They have discovered an important point that others may never figure out . . . NEVER SHUT DOWN THE BUYING MACHINE!

This brings to mind a friend from Atlanta, Steve Jordan. In January 1992, Steve was working for IBM. In February that year, he attended our Ft. Lauderdale Boot Camp because his intentions were to go full-time into real estate and he wanted to get a jump start.

That's exactly what he got. He recently wrote that he netted more than $64,000 on just four deals in the first five months of his full-time career.

One deal in particular sticks in my mind. Steve paid $32,000 for a house worth about $60,000. the house needed about $6,000 to $8,000 in repairs. He repaired it and sold it retail for a $16,000 profit. Later, he discovered the seller had paid only $15,000 for the house. That's a $17,000 easy profit to Steve's seller and a $16,000 profit to Steve all on the same house.

Who says this is the stuff of fairy tales?

"Leverage Your Brain First...
Money Last."

ANONYMOUS

Each problem has hidden in it an opportunity so powerful that it literally dwarfs the problem. The greatest success stories were created by people who recognized a problem and turned it into an opportunity.

Joseph Sugerman

Chapter **7**

Assumptions: Using Non-Qualifying Loans

I know from all my experience in buying houses that beginning investors can make good money quickly on assumption deals. I have found this to be one of the easiest and quickest methods of buying and selling a property in weeks, days, or even hours. Using this technique, you will find loans that can be assumed, such as non-qualifying FHA and VA loans, or you can create non-qualifying financing by using seller financing.

The beauty of this is that non-qualifying loans require little money and no credit checks, and you need very little training to do them. A non-qualifying loan is any loan that does not contain a "due-on-sale" clause. (Due-on-sale gives the lender the right to call the loan due when the property transfers ownership.) The absence of this clause takes control away from the lender and makes the loan freely assumable with or without the lender's permission. This creates attractive financing because the buyer does not have to qualify for a new loan to buy the house. If a buyer can satisfy the seller's need for a cash down payment, he or she can buy a house regardless of their credit or inability to qualify under normal standards.

You must get into these deals with very little cash. In fact, you can even buy these with no money down. Sometimes, owners are two or three months behind on the payments, and you just pay the back payments and take over the loan. Often, you can sell the property before you have to take title to it. If you find a buyer before you close, you can often have the property deeded directly to the new buyer and just pick up a check for the difference. If you buy a property for $1,000 down and sell it for $4,000 down, you keep the fast $3,000 profit.

Here is an example of an assumption deal that was located by my son-in-law, Bobby. Before I tell you about the deal, maybe I should tell you about Bobby.

When he was in his twenties, he had hair down to his shoulder blades. His main ambition in life was to be a rock-and-roll star. That's right, one of those hippie-looking, guitar-banging, noisy rock stars. Now, I don't have a problem with that so long as I don't have to listen to the racket; it drives me up the wall. Hey, a man's gotta do what he likes, right?

Anyway, over the years, Bobby has become proficient at putting together deals when he decides he wants to work, which usually happens only after he runs out of money. Not long ago, a couple called about our ad that we buy houses. They had a house with a $50,000 FHA loan that was assumable with no qualifying, and they wanted $2,000 cash in addition.

Bobby looked at the house and determined that it was in good condition and worth in the mid-$50s. He knew from experience that the less he gave the seller, the more he would make when he found a buyer. He had learned that the only way he could make quick cash on an assumption was to get in with little or nothing down, then find a buyer who would bring a few thousand dollars to the closing and assume the loan without qualifying. He could keep the difference between what his buyer paid down and what he had to give to the seller.

He tried to convince the sellers to deed the house to him. He said he would take over the loan and pay the closing costs, but they wouldn't bite. However, they did agree to accept $1,000 at closing.

Within two weeks, Bobby had found a buyer with $5,000 and set up a closing for a few days later. From *that $5,000, he paid the sellers the $1,000 and put $4,000 in his pocket.*

While that wasn't a big deal, it was a fast, easy $4,000 any way you look at it. I forgot to tell you why Bobby wanted this deal. You see, I was about to take a trip to Las Vegas for a speaking engagement, and Bobby and my daughter Vicki wanted to come along. The only way they could afford this was to work a deal such as I've just described. As I said before, Bobby really works when a sense of urgency strikes him.

Incidentally, all the money was gone within 24 hours of landing in Vegas! Oh well, easy come, easy go.

With this type of deal, I recommend that the house be in excellent condition. You also profit most by getting into this property with the least possible down payment. The holding costs can be held to a minimum through negotiation with the seller. For example, if you bought the house in the middle of the month, and the seller expects to be in the house through the start of the next month, you can reasonably ask him to make the next month's payment, thus reducing holding costs and increasing your profits.

This is typical of a retail assumption deal that generates immediate capital. If the house appraised for $55,000, you could still sell it for $56,000, $57,000, or even $58,000 if you wish. The financing makes the house very attractive to the buyer and, consequently, makes the house worth more. In either case, you have no reason to appraise the house and neither will your buyer. It's worth whatever you say it's worth.

But what if the buyer does not have $5,000 cash for a down payment? You can take whatever down payment he has and payments in the form of a second mortgage until it is paid off with interest. Or, let them rent the house until they have paid the entire $5,000 over and above their payment, then deed the house to them.

Six Keys to Successful Assumption Deals

1. The house must be in good condition, needing few, if any, repairs. You shouldn't spend more than $1,000 to upgrade and purchase a $50,000 property.

2. Pass by any deal if you can't get into it with only a small investment of cash. If it doesn't fit your guidelines, WALK AWAY. There are hundreds of other deals that DO fit.

On the other hand, don't walk away without leaving an offer. If the seller becomes motivated enough in the future, he may decide that your offer looks pretty good after all.

The monthly payment on any assumption should be about 1% of the original loan. For example, an $80,000 loan should have a monthly payment of about $800. Similarly, a $55,000 loan should have payments of no more than $550 a month. You would have a problem selling a $55,000 house with a $750 monthly payment.

People living in $100,000 homes are accustomed to paying $1,000 a month. This type of transaction will work on a $150,000 house as well as a $50,000 house. However, with the more expensive homes, it is even more important to watch your carrying costs and enter into the transaction with very little risk.

3. The property must have an assumable non-qualifying loan, or you must have a good working knowledge of seller financing to create it yourself. Creating seller financing is discussed in Chapter 13. It is an excellent means of creating income.

4. **Ask for the right amount of down payment when reselling the house.** I try to match carefully the amount of down payment with what I know about my potential buyer. If you are selling a $150,000 house, then you would expect $10,000 to $20,000 down. Is that too much? Not really. I know from experience that people who would live in a $150,000 home usually have that amount of money to put down. For a $50,000 house, however, you may not be able to get more than $5,000 down. It is usually difficult to get more than a 10% down payment, so a good rule of thumb would be to keep it to 10% or less.

5. **Let your buyer pay all the closing costs.** Just write it into the sales contract and act as though it's normal. The contract determines who pays what closing costs. Remember, buyers of assumptions often can't qualify at the bank, so they tend to be a lot less picky than buyers who can qualify. You are in control, so you make the rules.

6. **Try not to take title to the house.** Ideally, you will have resold the house prior to the closing. As mentioned above, if you find a seller who needs $1,000 to get out of his problem, and you find a buyer who has $4,000 to put down, you can set up a simultaneous closing and make $3,000. If you close and take title, however, you then become responsible for the payments and closing costs. Of course, I would recommend that you always have the house under contract before you try to market it, and you should be prepared to close even if you can't find a buyer before your contract expires.

When you become proficient at finding a buyer first and then find the house to buy, the entire process becomes much easier. I have done many of these assumption deals. Some I had to buy first; on others, I did a simultaneous closing with the new buyer and seller present at the same closing. In that case, all I had to do was pick up my check and look for another good deal.

Either way will work, but your profit will be smaller if you actually take title, because you will probably pay some or all of the closing costs and some holding costs.

TYPES OF LOANS TO SEEK

It is best to look for assumable non-qualifying loans. Those are VA loans closed prior to March 1, 1988, FHA loans closed prior to December 15, 1989, and most private loans that do not contain a due-on-sale clause. VA and FHA loans closed after those dates also can be assumed, but they require qualifying because there is a due-on-sale clause attached to them. This is time consuming and does not fit into our program very well.

Make sure you find out when the loan on a particular property closed. Get in the habit of asking when the owners closed the loan when you take the information over the phone. Assumable private loans also can work very well for investors because they can be below normal interest rates and require no points and other fees to assume.

Thousands of houses with good, non-qualifying FHA and VA loans are available. This means that you just have to be alive to assume the loan. There are no other requirements. Simply take over the loan and make the payments. A corporation, a trust, or any other entity can buy such properties. If there are two homes on the market, one with a non-qualifying loan and the other requiring a new loan, the assumption will sell faster every time. I have seen deals like this in every city to which I have traveled.

You don't have to steal assumptions. You can buy them for what they are worth or a little less. I'm talking about buying them for 80%, 90%, or even 100% of their value and still making money. What makes them worthwhile is the loan. It doesn't require lender's credit checks or other qualifying requirements. It's all in the financing. You can use this technique over and over again to make money. It's an easy-in, easy-out method.

Most old FHA or VA loans may be assumed for a $45-$125 transfer fee. However, do not assume the loan under your own name. Assume it under a trust or corporate name (see Chapter 14 on taking title and land trusts). This will avoid personal liability.

Failure is not an option. It's just the nagging possibility that helps you stay focused.

Anonymous

Chapter

Lease Options: Taking Control Without Taking Title

The fourth way I make quick profits on houses is to use a lease option or just an option. Anyone can cash in big by controlling property while never taking title. This method will work on houses in any condition, in any price range, and with any kind of underlying financing. You can reap large profits without ever owning the house. You don't have to pay any closing costs or do any repairs. You use little or no money and take no risk. There are two versions of this technique.

LEASED TO YOU, SUBLEASED TO YOUR TENANT

In the first version, I lease with option to buy and reserve the right to sublease to a tenant/buyer, who will eventually buy from me. There are three profit centers involved in this kind of transaction. Since I have the right to sublease, or sandwich lease, the first profit will be made the day I put a tenant in the house. The objective is to get a non-refundable down payment or earnest money deposit from my tenant/buyer. This will always be more than I gave the seller to secure my lease option, because one of the criteria for this kind of deal is to obtain control of the house with little or no cash. It's non-refundable because I have made it perfectly clear to my tenant/buyer that if he doesn't buy the house, he won't get a refund.

For example, if I gain control of a house in good condition, give the seller $1,000 and get $3,000 from a tenant/buyer a few days later, I have made an instant $2,000 for renting the house. Pay attention all you readers who need money two weeks from Friday. What I have just told you could be a full-time business, producing $10,000 per month income simply by renting three or four houses you don't even own.

The second avenue of income is the monthly spread I will attempt to create between the amount I collect from my tenant/buyer and the amount I pay my seller to cover his payments. This is raw profit that is also non-refundable. For example, if I am collecting $650 a month and paying $450 a month, I receive $200 a month profit for collecting rent on a house I don't own. That beats the 10% REALTORS® collect, doesn't it?

OK, I know what you're thinking. You're concerned that you need a license to do this, aren't you? Wrong! As long as you have a lease option agreement signed by the seller, you need no license of any kind. This gives you an equitable interest in the house, giving you the right to sell or lease the house without being licensed. In fact, you don't have to be licensed to use any of the strategies and techniques I teach. You don't need a license to buy or sell houses as long as you have them under contract to purchase or option, and your purchase is not contingent on selling the house before you buy it. Let's just keep it simple and successful.

Another advantage of collecting earnest money and a monthly spread is that it's not taxable as income until your buyer either buys the house or defaults, as long as you call it all "option money" and not "rent received."

The third income generator is the spread between the price you negotiate as your buying price and the amount for which you actually sell the house when your tenant/buyer exercises his option to purchase. This could be a substantial sum and frequently is much more than you would make if you actually took title.

Remember, you have only optioned the house. You haven't actually agreed to purchase it. An option is a unilateral agreement giving you control without forcing you to buy. Therefore, if things don't work out as planned, you can back out with no loss.

LEASE OPTION WITHOUT THE SUBLEASE

What you are about to read in the next few paragraphs is known to only a handful of people in the entire country. This method itself could become a full-time endeavor. If you become adept at marketing houses, what I'm about to tell you could enable you to make $200,000 this year. You need little money, no credit, no partner, no employees, and you'll do no repairs on a house. In fact, you can work in middle- and upper-class neighborhoods if you like, deal only with the cream of the crop, and make no monthly payments in the process.

Before you get too excited, let me emphasize that the key to being successful is to become proficient at marketing houses. First, look for the areas with the most sales activity in any price range. If they're selling fast, I don't care how much they're selling for. Actually, the higher the price, the better, because the higher the values, the more room you have to negotiate a wider spread.

Next, do everything possible to find all the houses for sale in these neighborhoods. Use several of the techniques described in Chapter 9 to find motivated sellers. You're looking for houses in excellent condition, in very marketable areas, and preferably vacant, because they'll be easier to show. These houses must have at least enough equity to make it worth your while to sell them. If they're fully financed, they may work for the lease/sublease method, but not for this one. Use your Property Acquisition Worksheet to determine whether this is a worthwhile opportunity for you, or a deal you should ignore.

Your objective is to find sellers with problems other than necessary major house repairs. For example:

- The owner has moved and still has mortgage payments.
- The house needs minor work (that you're willing to do).
- The seller wants all cash at closing and won't compromise, but will sell below market value.
- The seller hasn't been able to sell because of poor sales techniques. or the REALTOR® is lazy, or nobody is ever around to answer the phone, etc.

Many other circumstances create flexible sellers as well. In this case, your seller doesn't have to be all that motivated because you don't have to be rigid to make a profitable deal. Your main concern is to negotiate a purchase price far enough below market value to make it worth your while to get involved.

The goal is to option the house below market value, sell it at or near market value, then keep the difference.

Let's see how this works in real life. The seller calls me and says he has a house for sale at $125,000, in a lovely area and in excellent condition. He owes $87,000 on the house, has a conventional loan with a due-on-sale clause, would like to leave town in 60 days, but he has to sell before going. He is very credit conscious and won't sign a deed until his loan is paid off and he gets his equity, or at least some of it. This might be our conversation:

Q. "Mr. Seller, you say you want $125,000 and you think that's about what the house is worth. Is that correct?"
A. *"Yes."*

Q. "You say you need cash and debt relief on a non-assumable loan. The only way I may be able to help you is with our lease option plan where I can cash you out if we can agree on a price and if your house qualifies. It might take me a few months to pay you, but it would be in cash. Would you like to hear about it?"
A. *"Yes."*

Q. "Actually, it's quite simple. There are two different ways we can work it. One, I can lease your house with the right to sublease to a tenant/buyer who should eventually buy the house. The downside to this, of course, is that someone will be living in the house. The upside is that your payment will be made in the process. The second way I can help you is to option your house at a price we both can live with and leave it vacant until I sell it. I have a good supply of buyers who want to live in your

area and, frankly, I don't feel it would take long to sell it. The downside is if I don't have the right to sublease, then I can't make your payment while I'm selling the house. Which option sounds best to you?"

A. *"I don't want anyone tearing up my house."*

Q. "I don't blame you and I couldn't honestly guarantee you that that wouldn't happen if I put a tenant/buyer in the house. I can prescreen them, but I can't live with them."

A. *"You mean you want to take my house off the market and not even pay a monthly payment?"*

Q. "Yes, Mr. Seller, that is one of your options. Let's examine it a little further. First, who's making the payment now?"

A. *"I am, of course."*

Q. "Who will be making it six months from now if the house doesn't sell?"

A. *"I guess I will."*

Q. "Exactly! Now, let's examine the part about taking your house off the market. I can see where this could be a concern. You don't know I'm going to do anything for sure, do you?"

A. *"I sure don't."*

Q. "Then let's do it this way. I'll option your house and give it my best efforts. I'll advertise at my expense. I'll eat, sleep, smell, touch, taste, and feel your house until it's sold. It will be on my mind day and night. In fact, since I'm not a REALTOR® with 25 other houses to sell, it will be my only concern until it's sold. All I need from you is an agreement on the price and a key. Are you with me so far?"

A. *"Yes! But you still haven't convinced me that I should take it off the market."*

Q. "I understand your concern, but what if you don't take it off the market? What if you continue doing what you're doing now to sell it? If you get a buyer before I do, simply cut me a check at closing for $1,000 to cover my time and expenses and we'll part friends. Is that reasonable?"

A. "You mean if I sell it first, I can buy your option for $1,000?"

Q. "Yes, Mr. Seller, that's exactly what I mean. I want you to be in a no-risk situation. It's whichever way you win first."

A. "Why should I pay you $1,000 if I sell the house myself?"

Q. "Mr. Seller, quite frankly, if we can't agree on that, then maybe your house isn't the one I should be devoting my money and effort to selling. It comes down to a simple choice. Do you want someone else aggressively selling your house or do you want to continue fighting the battle yourself? I would think that with a buyout of a measly $1,000, it would be well worth a shot at it, don't you?"

A. "Well, why don't I just list it with a REALTOR®?"

Q. "I have no problem with that, if you're convinced it will help. You can list the house with a REALTOR® while still giving me the option. If the REALTOR® sells first, I'll back off and you only owe me $1,000. However, you should know that if I sell your house first, which is a very real possibility, you will still be responsible for the REALTOR'S® commission, unless you ask the REALTOR® to exclude me. Most REALTORS® are willing to do that if you ask. That simply means they won't get paid if I sell the house first. Why don't you give me just 60 days before listing? If I haven't found a buyer in that length of time, then go ahead and list and I'll even waive the $1,000. Is that fair?"

A. "Yes! That sounds very reasonable."

Q. "Good. Do you think we have a basis for doing business?"

A. *"Yes!"*

Q. "Great! The only thing left is for me to come look and for us to agree on a price. I think I've made it clear that I have to buy below market value to get involved. You are going to be flexible on your price aren't you?"

A. *"Well, just how flexible?"*

Q. "As I said, I can't pay full price. The only way I can make a profit is to buy well below market value. I can't say just how much until I see the house, but I'm telling you before I come out there that I will need a low price to get involved. Before I leave, you'll know what I can pay. Should I come look?"

A. *"Sure! I'd be pleased to have you come on out. I do need to get the house sold."*

I suggest that you go back over this conversation a few times until it becomes perfectly clear what I have done. Look at the questions and answers carefully. This is the way to get what you want from the seller. You should also practice dialogues like this with someone willing to help. You don't want a seller to think this is your first deal, so practice a little. Practice without pressure, and you will feel more confident when you're in front of the seller. It won't take the butterflies out of your stomach, but it will get them flying in formation.

There it is in a nutshell. I have taken control of a lovely home in a nice neighborhood with no money down, no monthly payments, and no closing costs, at a price below market and with no repairs to make. In addition, I've agreed to do nothing but attempt to sell a house and have no liability if I don't. I've put the seller in a no-lose situation, and agreed to pay all cash for the house when I buy.

In the process, I've given the seller the choice of whether he wants his payments made. Either way, I win.

If the seller chooses to leave the house vacant, I won't make the payment. If he allows me to sublease the property, I will make the payment if the house qualifies. He decides. Just think for a moment. All I'm asking the seller to do, if he chooses the vacant route, is to give me a key to show the house and agree on a purchase price. That's it.

I've put the seller in a no-risk situation with positive possibilities without even taking his house off the market. Just how hard do you think you'll have to look to find people who own nice, vacant houses in lovely areas, and who are willing to sell a little below market value for all cash with no risk? I suspect you know the answer to that question . . . SUCH PEOPLE ARE EVERYWHERE!

Now, my only role is to find a buyer for the house and help the buyer find financing. He or she will bring a check to closing. My seller will be there to get his share after his loan is paid off, and I'll leave with the difference. If I could get my seller to reduce his sales price from $125,000 to $110,000, which, by the way, would be about the most I would pay, I would realize a $15,000 profit on a house I don't own.

I would expect my seller to pay about half the closing costs and my buyer to pay the other half. That leaves yours truly with no costs except advertising.

This is the basic approach to lease options. I have only begun to show you what is possible using this strategy. I have much, much more to share with you, but that is another whole course.

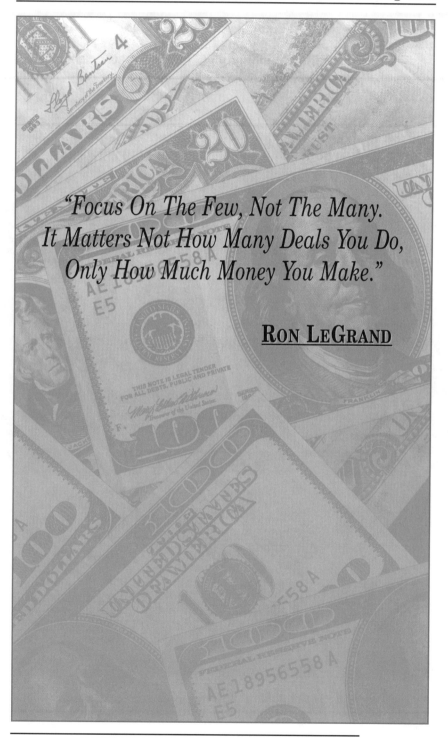

"Focus On The Few, Not The Many.
It Matters Not How Many Deals You Do,
Only How Much Money You Make."

RON LEGRAND

Section III
Smart Marketing

Most people give up just when
they're about to achieve success;
they quit on the one yard line.
They give up at the last minute
of the game, one foot from
a winning touchdown.

H. Ross Perot

Chapter

Finding Motivated Sellers

Finding motivated sellers is vital to your success. A motivated seller is the key to all good deals. Read this sentence again and burn it into your brain forever. It will lead you to increase your profits, make better deals, put more cash in your pocket, and save valuable time. You must learn to understand and identify motivated sellers, or all the other information in this book will be useless. You'll spend all your time chasing dead ends and getting nowhere. And you won't be in this business very long.

Motivation comes in all forms. Some reasons relate to the owners themselves, such as divorce, age, health problems, or a change in family size. Others are more directly related to the property itself. Maybe it needs extensive repairs. In other cases, an owner might be having financial problems, be behind in his payments, or even on the verge of foreclosure.

One of the primary reasons for the failure of a deal is trying to buy from unmotivated sellers. It's like trying to push a rope. It will absorb all your time and energy and will get you nowhere. **Find the seller who really wants to sell**, and you will buy a lot more houses at far better prices. The secret to great deals is to find them before anyone else does.

The **first** thing you must do is let the world know you're in the house business. If you were arrested, would they have enough evidence against you to convict you of dealing in houses? Are you ashamed of being a real estate investor, or are you shouting it to the world?

Don't rely on just one or two methods to get the word out. You should pick at least five ways to find houses and put all five methods to work simultaneously. Remember, you want to make yourself prone to success. The more you put yourself in the way of opportunity, the better your chances of getting what you want.

This is important because if you try to do business only one way and don't find a house in a short time, you'll become frustrated or discouraged and quit. By knowing this from the start, you can avoid falling short and missing out on a fortune. Accept the fact that you have to do more than run an ad and sit back and wait for motivated sellers to call you to come take their houses.

To be honest, if that's all you did, you could still make a living, but you aren't after a living here, are you? You want retirement, fat city, a hammock in sunny Tahiti, travel, no debt, and all the money you can spend, don't you? If that's true, let's treat this like a business and use more than one way to attract customers. The more lines you cast into the pond, the better chance of getting a bite. If you use at least several of the following methods, you will receive more calls from motivated sellers than you can handle. That's right! The sellers will be calling you!

Why is it so important that the seller call you? Because they are always more motivated when they call you first. Knowing this, I suggest you do everything possible to encourage people to call you. Don't spend a lot of time dealing with unmotivated sellers who are just testing the waters.

Following are 15 tools that will aid you in your search for the sellers you need. Use them all, if you can. But experience has shown that you must use at least five simultaneously to succeed.

CARDS

Cards are the least expensive, most effective way to advertise. They will cost between $15 and $75 per thousand, depending on how fancy they are and the kind of paper you use. A lot of your cards will be thrown out. Sorry, but that's real life. Some of them will be saved, and a few will generate a phone call right away.

Here's the bonus question: How many deals do you have to do to pay for your cards? One single card is going to do it. The catch is, you never know which card. Don't be shy about giving out cards and telling everyone what you are doing. Even someone who has absolutely no interest in buying or selling a house might know of others who ARE interested. EVERYONE is either a prospect or a potential source of referrals.

Cards won't do you any good in the box, so hand them out everywhere, to everyone you meet. Leave them in restaurants, barber shops, stores, offices, and wherever else you go. Put them in the envelopes when you pay your local bills. If you have 1,000 cards more than three months, you're not getting the best use from them.

The message on the card should say something like "I **BUY HOUSES, CASH, ANY CONDITION." "I BUY & SELL HOUSES"** also gets a lot of attention. To get double impact from your cards, reprint the message from your flyer on the back.

Make your cards as outstanding as possible. Be different! My card is a bright fluorescent orange. It really attracts attention. People want to keep it because it is unique. When I visit business acquaintances, I often spot my card in their card file, even years later. You might consider using those fancy, four-color, glossy, picture cards. They're expensive, but highly effective.

Your card is a billboard to telegraph your message. Be crystal clear about what you do. Avoid phrases like "Real Estate Investor." That means nothing to a motivated seller. People are only interested in what you can do for them.

RUN ADS

The easiest way to find motivated sellers is to run ads in your local newspapers and let the sellers call you. Which papers? As many as possible. Most of the calls you get will be worthless, but you only need a good one once in a while to make a good income.

You don't need fancy wording or displays to get calls. The ad I have used for years simply says, "We buy houses, fast cash, two-day closing, any condition, any price, phone number." I use a bold headline and avoid crowding my ads. I usually run ads in the "Real Estate Wanted" section. Run your ad in different sections of the paper to see what works in your area. Only practice will tell you what is most effective.

Don't be concerned about the competition advertising in the paper. It's amazing, but even when eight or 10 ads, all saying the same thing, run side by side, we all get calls. Quite often, they're not the same calls, either. Most people will call only one or two ads. But if your phone number is in their area, or there is something in your ad they like, your number is one they'll dial.

READ ADS

The other side of the coin is to call ads yourself. I recommend calling ads that are in the major newspapers, as well as those in shoppers and neighborhood papers.

Don't think there are no good deals in the papers just because many people read them. First, most investors check only a few ads before giving up. Second, you know exactly what to look for, so your search for leads will be much more effective. With assumption-type deals, look for ads that say "no qualifying," "assumption," or something to that effect. For buy low-sell high retail deals, look for wording such as "as-is," "make offer," "estate sale," "needs work," "handyman special," or "investor special."

When calling or answering ads, complete an information sheet to help you remember the details about each property, and to help you decide if the property fits into one of your purchase categories: buy low-sell high, loan assumption, or lease option. Why didn't I mention buy low-sell low here? Because any house that qualifies as a retail house will also qualify as a wholesale house. The difference lies in what you do with it after putting it under contract. You will either retail the house to a homeowner or wholesale it to another investor.

The following is an example of what you might say when calling to answer an ad. I have these conversations every day, first on the phone and then at the property.

ON THE TELEPHONE

"I'm calling about your ad in the paper. I see you have a house in (city), you have a mortgage on it of about $54,000, and you are asking for $5,000 down. Will you tell me a little about the house?"

The seller describes the house to you.

"I'm an investor, and I'm looking for houses in your area. I'm very serious, but I can tell you before I come over that I can't pay you $5,000 down on that house. I have to make a profit to be interested in looking at your home, and that just wouldn't be possible if I gave you your full $5,000. If I come over, I will leave you with an offer, but I can tell you before I come that it won't be anywhere near what you're asking. Should I come look?"

"Yes."

If the seller says yes, then skip ahead to the question about loan assumability. But if the seller says no . . .

"I can understand that. If I was in your position, I would want to get all I could, as well. However, would you take my name and telephone number and let me know if things don't work out as planned, so we can get together?"

Leave the door open. You can sometimes get these houses by putting yourself in the second position. If the seller can't find his ideal buyer, then you want to be second in line to buy the property. A lot of houses have been bought using this technique, so remember to use it whenever you have to.

"If the loan is assumable, when did you close on it?"

The date the seller gives us confirms that the loan is assumable without qualifying.

"Tell me how to find your house, and we'll set up an appointment right now so I can look at it. I'll see you at 3 p.m., and I'll let you know what I can do before I leave. By the way, will you and your wife both be home then?"

You must have all owners present because both sellers must sign the contract for the property to change hands.

AT THE HOUSE

"You have a nice house here. It looks like it's in pretty good shape. Your payment is OK; the only problem I have is that I can't give you what you are requiring down. The best I can do is give you $1,000 down, cash to mortgage, and pay your closing costs. Would that be of interest?"

"I want $2,500 cash down, Ron."

"I'd love to give it to you! And you know what, I think you can probably get it, if you want to leave the house on the market until somebody comes along who wants to live in it. I just can't give it to you because what I'm going to do with your house is find that buyer you're looking for, and I've got to have a way to make a profit. If I were selling your house as a REALTOR®, would I make a commission? It's only fair that I make one if I do it as a non-REALTOR®, right? If I give you more than $1,000, then I just wouldn't be able to profit from my efforts. Can you see my point?"

"Well, I guess so, Ron."

"The only way I can do that is if I give you $1,000, get $3,000 from a buyer, and make a profit. If that will work for you, I can do it. If not, you're not mad at me, are you, Mr. Seller? I told you before I came over that I was going

to leave you with an offer, didn't I? OK, I'm leaving you with an offer of $1,000 down, and I'll pay your closing costs. I've got to buy some houses by the end of the week, so that offer is only going to be good for another three days."

The probability of the seller's taking this offer is 50/50. He might accept the offer on the spot, wait a couple of days before calling you back, or just say, "no." I do not leave a written offer unless the seller is ready to sign it. This saves time and keeps the seller from having REALTORS® pick my contract apart. I suggest that you write on a piece of paper: "$1,000, cash to mortgage, plus closing cost, and your name, address, and phone number."

If, in the phone conversation, the seller says that he will not take less than $5,000 down, I leave him my name and phone number and tell him to call if a time comes when we should get together. Why go look at houses you know you can't buy? Prequalify the seller before you leave home. Remember, you only work with motivated sellers.

FSBO SIGNS

It's amazing how many people do not advertise the house they want to sell. Some people are so sure the world will beat a path to their door that they just put up a single, small, hand-made sign, one that sometimes is not even visible from the street. Of course, this can work to your advantage as an investor. If you are the only one who pays any attention, you are also the only one to make an offer. Poorly advertised FSBO homes are excellent prospects for Quick-Turn deals.

Write down the telephone number if it's on the sign, call the owner, and get the information about the house. Better still, get out of the car and knock on the door. Fill out a Property Information Sheet and see if you can make a deal that falls into one of our four categories. If there's no telephone number on the sign, even better! Just knock on the front door and start talking.

Always look for FSBO signs when you're driving around. Take a different route home each day, and make it a point to cruise the neighborhoods looking for deals. Neighborhoods change every day, and so do the houses for sale

REFERRALS

Would it benefit you to have 10 people searching for deals on your behalf? How about 100 people? Could you afford to pay them all? The answer is yes! You certainly can afford to pay someone $250 when they bring you a deal that makes you $10,000 or $20,000 in a short time.

Such people are called "bird dogs," and they are a fine source of leads you otherwise would not hear about. It doesn't matter how many bird dogs you have working for you, because you only pay them when you actually close on a good deal. You can mention in all your ads that you also pay $250 for leads, and you'll end up with more bird dogs than you can possibly handle. If you're a serious investor, you should always get people to bird dog for you.

Why would anyone be a bird dog? Why wouldn't they buy the deal themselves? The answer is simple. They lack knowledge! They didn't buy this book, so they believe they can't do a deal because of lack of money, lack of confidence in themselves, and a dozen other reasons. They see being a bird dog as something they can do.

The person seeking out houses for you doesn't need to make any loans or apply for credit. He just has to have a car to find the FSBOs and vacant and run-down houses. All he has to do is collect information. When dealing with vacant houses, he must get the owner's name, address, and phone number to get the $250 at closing. Bird dogs get only $100 without the owner's information. In some cases, you can pay more. This arrangement can be lucrative for both you and your bird dogs. Put them to work! It doesn't cost you a dime unless they bring you a deal that you can turn into cash.

To save their time and yours, educate your bird dogs about your requirements for a good deal. Give them a Bird Dog Sheet and a Property Information Sheet, found in Appendices C and D. They are self-explanatory and easy to complete.

Ask everyone you talk to if they know of anyone selling a house. Tell them that if you buy a house they have referred to you, you will pay them $250 at closing. Let the word get around town that you pay for leads, and you may soon have more than you can handle.

It's possible that you might get some flack from overzealous REALTORS® who think this activity is illegal, because the bird dogs don't have a license. In my opinion, however, you are simply paying for information, since the bird dogs are not performing any of the functions of a REALTOR®.

Let's talk about another method of bird dogging. This one will require a little money out of pocket, but it will bring in more leads than you can process. In fact, if you used this method and nothing else, you could buy five houses a month from it and it alone.

Here's how it works. Instead of paying your bird dogs only after you close on a deal, why not pay them the minute they bring you leads? Let's say you tell 10 people that you will pay them $10 for each lead they furnish about vacant houses in poor condition, provided they supply addresses and 35 mm photos, as well. These houses may or may not be listed with REALTORS®. They might or might not have a sign.

Would you pay $100 for 10 of these kinds of leads? You bet you would. Gladly! That's a small price to pay to get others to do all the driving around while you sit in your office and process the information.

If you train your people to find what you're looking for, and pay only for qualified leads, you'll see that your minimum outgo will produce maximum results. If you're furnished 20 houses that look bad and are vacant, you should be able to buy at least one or two of them and make anywhere from $5,000 to $25,000 or more in profit. Would you pay $200 to make $25,000? Tough question, huh?

FLYERS

I love this one. Flyers are even better than direct mail. Design an 8 1/2" by 11" flyer and distribute it door to door in neighborhoods where you want to buy. I promise, if you distribute 3,000 to 4,000 flyers in this manner, you'll be quite pleased with the results. I don't believe I've ever done that and not bought a house as a result.

The best part is that the flyer can last for years and produce results when you least expect them. Remember the house mentioned in Chapter 4? The one on which I made $23,000 from a year-and-a-half-old flyer?

Basically, the flyer should read like your ad. Don't crowd it; just get the message across. You can hire students or people from your local labor board to distribute them. Two people can put out 500 flyers in three hours. Put flyers on every door in the neighborhood. This beats all other forms of advertising, because you know it was delivered where you wanted it to be and that it got read.

Do stay out of trouble. Avoid car windows and mail boxes: they are off limits. People don't like to see strangers touching their cars; it is a kind of invasion of privacy. And it's against federal law to put anything but the U.S. Mail in a mailbox.

VACANT HOUSES

Whenever you canvass the neighborhood with flyers, you'll also want to be on the lookout for vacant houses and check them out. Vacant houses make motivated sellers and good bargains. They probably aren't even on the market. And few people are willing to hunt for them, so you will have little or no competition.

Telltale signs that a house is vacant: the lawn is not cared for and weeds have begun to take over, the postman may be bypassing the house with the junk mail; the paper boy is no longer delivering; there may be a pile of papers in front, and more than one old coupon flyer may be attached to the doorknob. After looking for vacant houses for a while, you'll begin to see the pattern and spot these properties even faster. Record addresses of vacant houses, then check with the neighbors for the whereabouts of the owners and information regarding a way to get in touch with them.

If the neighbors can't tell you how to contact the owners, be sure to keep whatever information you have collected. After you have six to 10 addresses of vacant houses, go to the courthouse and look up the owners of each. Each courthouse is set up a little differently, so just ask for help from the clerks in the office that handles tax revenues and plat maps.

They are generally very helpful and willing to guide you through the particular system used in their office, if you ask politely and act humble.

Another way to find house owners is to subscribe to a data service whose database contains the tax rolls and is accessible via your computer.

Send owners of these houses a flyer or letter. If the owner's address and the vacant house address are the same, send a first class letter. If it is first class, it may get forwarded to them. But before you mail a flyer, you should definitely leave one at the house itself, because people sometimes come back to their houses. Even if the owner does not come back, someone who is in contact with him might appear. Leave at least two or three flyers at the vacant house, since there is also a chance a neighbor will take one.

Another way to find out who owns a vacant house is to go to the post office and find out if there is a forwarding address for the property. There is a $3 charge for this information, but you often can learn the name and current address of whoever was living there last. It's worth a try.

Obviously, not all the letters you send to owners of vacant houses will lead somewhere. But a few will. And if one or two of these leads turn into a deal in a three-month period, you can make a fair living.

As an added bonus, if the vacant house is in an estate, an attorney for the family will receive the mail. He may direct you to even more properties.

We conducted a Boot Camp in Pittsburgh and one of the students was a young man from there named Robert Hunter. Bob had heard me speak at his local association meeting in Pittsburgh a few months earlier, and he had bought my course.

Needless to say, he got fired up with what he heard and quickly decided he wanted to get in the business. So, he registered for our Atlanta Boot Camp in July to get some fast, hands-on training. After attending that week, he went out and found some great deals on houses, but he hadn't learned to move fast enough yet. He knew he had found great deals, but he still hadn't cured his paralysis of analysis. While he was exploring all the angles, other real estate investors were buying the houses. He surely hadn't learned that nonsense from me. In fact, during the whole Boot Camp, I had pounded into him that you can't Quick-Turn in slow motion.

After a couple of tongue lashings from me over the phone for his screw-ups, Bob decided to pay a return visit to the Pittsburgh boot camp. He knew better than to come empty-handed with no leads or motivated sellers. He was fully aware that if he did I would grind him into the dirt during the entire camp.

One week before we arrived, he decided to go to work or face the consequences. During that week, he looked at several vacant houses and made an offer on two of them. While we were in session, he brought in a third one he had found; it was not only vacant — it was boarded up. He tracked down the owner and called from class to see if it was for sale, since there were no signs on the property.

We finally reached the son who had inherited the house and didn't know what to do with it. Bob asked him what he wanted for the house, and the reply was $5,000. Now that may not sound so great on a boarded-up house, but Bob had done his homework, and he knew the house was worth about $50,000 *repaired. Moreover, it didn't need more than $7,000 to $10,000 in work.*

To make a long story short, this young whipper - snapper made only three offers on three houses during that week, and all three were accepted. Bob was successful in buying about $125,000 worth of houses for a grand total of $30,000. The whole bunch didn't need more than $30,000 in repairs.

Bob quickly decided that he didn't have the money to buy or repair, so he sold the deals immediately to other investors and let them close on them. At last count, Bob figured to make about $20,000 cash on three deals he didn't buy.

I told this punk he was screwing up my averages. Nobody is supposed to make three offers and get three accepted. That's all right, Bob; don't play by the averages. Just go get filthy rich and tell me how wrong my averages were.

INVESTMENT GROUPS

There is an investment group or association in almost every major city in the country, as well as in many smaller cities. The sole purpose of these organizations is to educate real estate investors or would-be investors. Most are non-profit groups; they usually meet once a month. The meetings include varied activities and almost always present a speaker on some real estate-related subject. The members of these groups get together to learn new techniques, polish up old ones, share their knowledge with others, and stay motivated.

I've never met anyone who didn't need to have his or her batteries charged occasionally. There is no better venue for an investor to do that than at the monthly association meetings. In my opinion, they're an absolute must, if you're going to remain in the business, no matter how smart you are or think you are. The dues are minimal, and the information is free, current, and of immeasurable value. You will learn as much or more from the other members as you do from the speakers, and just being part of the group will help you avoid thousands of dollars in mistakes while helping you make thousands with what you learn.

Why am I bringing up groups when we are discussing how to locate good deals on houses? If the people in these groups are so educated, I am certainly not going to be able to pick up any good deals from them, am I? After all, they're in this for the same reason I am, aren't they? Wrong! That kind of thinking will cost you dearly. If you are retailing houses and not utilizing the group in your area, you are walking past a fortune.

All you have to do is let the group know you're looking for some good deals on houses and that you're a serious buyer. You'll have more deals to consider than you can handle. Try it and see for yourself. You'll soon discover that other members have different motivations than you do. There are people in that same room who would love to wholesale houses to three or four people like you as fast as they can find them. They can take a small, quick, cash profit and leave enough in the deal to satisfy the needs of a retailer like you. Usually, these folks prefer not to be in the house long enough to repair and market it to an owner/occupant. Their sole intent is to flip it in hours or days and go to the next one. They deal in volume and avoid anything complicated.

Wholesaling was covered in detail in Chapter 6. For now, trust me when I tell you that all the deals you can handle are as close as your next association meeting.

If you are in a group, but aren't active, get involved. You'll soon learn that the more you give of yourself, the better your return. You can't help someone up a hill without getting closer to the top yourself.

BANK AUCTIONS

Let's talk about auctions, which are an excellent source of leads. In fact, one of the best ways to get outrageous deals on houses is to attend auctions in which the lender is selling a batch of houses at the same time. These things are normally real fire sales. The foreclosures are piling up so fast the lenders can't keep up with the pace and often choose to "stack 'em high and sell 'em cheap."

You'll have plenty of advance notice of an auction if you watch the papers. Auctions are always advertised, usually in display ads and usually several times. You can order a brochure that contains all the pertinent information about the houses being sold. Sometimes everything you need to know is right in the newspaper.

You'll need some cash, or at least ready access to cash. All auctions require a deposit when you win a bid. Usually, this is 10% of the bid, but the amount may vary in different parts of the country. If you don't have the money, there are several ways to get it, but that's another chapter. In fact, that could be my next book. Those of you who can raise a deposit should keep your eyes open. Don't miss your next chance to get a smorgasbord of bargains.

One warning: You **MUST** inspect the houses before the auction. Under no circumstances should you bid for a house you haven't seen. The last time I did, it cost me $2,500 because I chose to forfeit the deposit rather than close the deal. The house needed a lot more work than the picture the auctioneer showed us. Inspect first, write down your absolute maximum bid, and stick to that amount at the auction. Don't let the auction frenzy sway your predetermined bid.

Buy the junkers! You are there for the great deals, not the good deals. Your target is all the houses in poor condition, not the ones in good shape and ready to occupy. Your competition for the pretty ones will be fierce from owner/occupants looking for a deal on their next residence or from unskilled investors who don't know where the real money is.

I remember attending an FDIC auction that was advertised in the local paper. About 30 houses had to be liquidated. The organizers rented a motel room and auctioned all the houses in one evening. More than 200 people were bidding on about 30 houses, yet when it came time for the junkers, fewer than 10 people were in the room bidding.

I had called previously for a brochure and gone to look at the ones I liked — the ugly ones. I've learned from experience that the odds of buying a pretty house at an auction, for a price I'm willing to pay, are pretty slim. I look for the worst-looking houses in the bunch, since I know there won't be many bidders on the ugly ducks.

Anyway, I bought two houses that night. Perhaps I should say I was the high bidder on two houses, because I never actually bought them. The high bid on one was $4,950. It was worth $32,000 after about $5,000 in repairs. The second one was worth about $42,000 and needed $8,000 in work. My high bid on it was $8,600.

Both houses looked bad, which is what had attracted me to them in the first place, but they were in saleable neighborhoods. I had to put 10% down that night for a total of $1,355. I then had 60 days to close with all cash.

The next day, I called a friend who was in the buy low-sell high business. I sold both houses to this young lady for $26,000 cash. In both cases, I never took title. A few days later, we were at the closing table. She had the $26,000, and I had the two contracts. While the title company was doing all the work, I sat there looking dumb while my buyer did all the signing and shelled out the cash.

I had the title company deed the house directly to my buyer. The seller wasn't even there. They just sent the packages to the closing agent with instructions. The closing agent took the $26,000 and subtracted the $13,550 that I had paid for both houses. The only thing for me to do was pick up a check and leave. That looks like $12,450 to me in a few short days without my ever taking title or touching those filthy houses. In fact, I never even went inside them. Man, this sure beats working for a living. Don't you just love it?

Don't feel sorry for my buyer. Yes, she will do a lot more work than I, and she has some capital outlay, but her profit on those two houses, when she sells them, will be in the neighborhood of $30,000 to $35,000 for both houses. And she will have it in hand within 90 days.

Ask me why my buyer wasn't at the auction. She could have saved $12,000 by being there, couldn't she? Yes, she could, but she didn't. Maybe there was an episode of *Seinfield* on TV that night that she didn't want to miss. Who knows? I'll let the psychologists figure out why people do the things they do.

Incidentally, you normally have 60 days to close if you are high bidder, and you should be able to find a buyer at a higher price within 60 days. The world is full of investors looking for bargains.

Of course, this is assuming you don't want to retail the houses yourself, as I sometimes get in the mood to do.

At a recent auction, I purchased a house for $18,700 cash. I paid the deposit and obtained a private investor loan for the balance. I spent $6,000 to repair it, and it appraised for $52,000 for a $25,000 profit. It's hard to beat those auction deals. Gosh, what if I did one of those every couple of months? How about one per month, or maybe one per week? Sounds crazy, huh?

I've turned more than 1,100 houses in 14 years. You figure out how many that is per month. While you're doing that, I'll be looking for another auction.

LENDERS

Lenders have inventories of houses they don't want, but were taken back through foreclosure. These houses are called "REOs," short for Real Estate Owned, or "repos," an abbreviated form of "repossessions." On the bank's financial statement, they point to other nastier names: liabilities, losses, non-conforming assets, failures, bad loans, and inept bank management. Needless to say, bankers hate REOs.

There are so many banks in most areas, it is best to concentrate on those that are really willing to deal with you. Not all will. Some banks want to recover just what was owed on the properties, while others may hope to obtain market value. However, some banks are willing to take losses, if necessary, to liquidate these REOs as fast as possible. They want to remove these embarrassments from their books. It is these you can buy even before they go up for auction. Make all-cash offers.

Buying from a lender can sometimes mean outrageous profits. One house I bought from a lender was sold by the bank at 17% of its true market value! However, you shouldn't worry about the percentages. In high-priced areas, 70% of the value can be a great deal, while in low-priced areas, 50% of the value may not be a good deal. Only the dollars are important, not the percentage of value.

You can work many types of deals when buying from lenders. Your best deals will be closed by paying all cash, but quite often the lenders are happy to create some financing for you with attractive terms, if you qualify.

MAILOUTS

Investors often neglect to obtain good mailing lists of potential, motivated sellers, because it appears to be impossible. Well, it is possible and very profitable! Although you may not be able to go to a list broker and say, "Give me the motivated sellers in this area," you can generate the list yourself.

First, go to your local courthouse and research all the divorce cases, out-of-state owners, houses with tax liens, mechanics' liens, pre-foreclosures, and Lis Pendens, which is the first step in a lawsuit. Also, as mentioned before, always stay on the lookout for vacant houses, or houses needing repairs.

Second, ask a REALTOR® to give you a list of expired listings with out-of-town owners. You can often make a deal with the Realtor who gives you the list. Tell them you will use them to make some offers, or simply offer to pay them for their services.

Mail all of the above names a letter and/or flyer. These people can be expected to be motivated. This will work with all expired listings, not just those belonging to out-of-towners

FHA/VA Repos

Most people are aware of these potential bargains, but they lack the knowledge to turn a mediocre deal into a good deal. If I were to offer the government's asking price when these houses first hit the market, I would be able to make a little money on some of them, but not enough to make me want to buy them. If this is true, then why do I bother with them? The answer is simple. I don't offer the price being asked! I offer what I am willing to pay!

Now wait a minute, Ron! My brother told me I have to offer the asking price because they won't accept a lower bid. That is true, but only while they are in the bid process. Let's review the process so we can get a better idea of the mechanics.

First, the houses we're talking about are all the FHA/VA foreclosures the lending institution holding the note elected not to keep themselves. Once the foreclosure process is complete, the house may be assigned to HUD or the to VA to liquidate. Or, the lender may now elect to keep it. In some cases, the assignment takes place before the foreclosure, and the government does the foreclosing.

It's totally irrelevant to me who forecloses. I'm only interested after the legal proceedings have ended and the house is on the market. That could take a year or more.

After the process is completed, a broker is hired to appraise the house and affix a value. Sometimes repairs are done, such as installing a new roof, in an attempt to make the house more marketable. Rarely will the repairs be extensive, and the house is almost never 100% renovated. Therefore, the value is usually below market value; sometimes it is considerably below.

Every once in a while, a property will become available so far below value that I'll jump on it at the price they are asking, but this is rare. Remember, I want only the good deals, not the mediocre ones.

Here's the key. If you are going to pick the pearls from this smorgasbord of wealth, you must wait until the initial bid period is up and deal only with the houses that were passed over.

These will be the clunkers, the yucks, the handyman specials, the real dirt bags. That's right! The uglier they are, the more they're worth to you. These are the ones all the owner/occupants passed up because they were so ugly. Remember, there are bucks in the yucks!

You must develop the ability to recognize opportunity and picture these houses in good shape. That ability is what will make you different from all the shortsighted people who passed up these deals.

What most investors don't know is that when the houses are placed on the "Extended Listing," the "Reduced for Quick Sale" listing, or the "Z" listing, you can offer any amount you want. The asking price will be published in the newspaper every week, along with the address and the number of bedrooms and baths.

All you have to do is take the list, look at the property, and decide what you are willing to offer. Will all your offers be accepted? I hope not. If they are, you offered too much. Somehow, I don't think that's a problem. I can assure you they won't all be accepted.

The worse the condition of the house, the better your chances are of getting a low offer accepted. The amount of time the house has been on the market is also a determining factor. It's tough to get these properties for much less than 80% of the asking price, but don't let that prevent you from making the offers. The worst thing that can happen is that your offer will be rejected.

On one occasion, I purchased a repo for 60% of the asking price; in reality, that was 20% of the after-repaired value. I sold that one for an instant $6,000 profit, without taking title or touching the house. As a matter of fact, I never even went inside it. You see, when I am buying a house for 20% of its value, I don't care if it has an inside. I bought another one for 85% of its asking price, and after spending $5,000 on repairs, I still was not involved for more than 55% of value.

Don't let these percentages fool you. In high-priced areas such as Los Angeles, Washington, D.C., and many others, you aren't going to get these houses at 50 cents on the dollar. Use common sense.

Again, it's only the dollars that count, not the percent of value. I have to buy at 20% to 50% of value dealing in the $35,000 to $55,000 range here in Jacksonville, Florida to make less money than do investors in Los Angeles who buy at 75% of value.

Here are some tips on how to make the offers. All areas have brokers who will submit offers for you. They have been trained on the forms and procedures and have a list of all the repos. I suggest that you seek one who specializes in HUD repos and work with him or her regularly. Not only have you added a professional to your team who knows the system, you also have someone to help you determine the value and marketability of the houses. Just don't forget that, even though the broker may seem friendly and well intentioned, his or her main concern is his or her commission check.

Each offer will require an earnest money deposit ranging from $500 in some areas to $2,000 in others. This is a nonrefundable deposit, so do your homework before you make the offer. Of course, if your offer isn't accepted, you will get a full refund.

If your offer is accepted, you will have up to 60 days to close or find someone else to close. Your broker may push you to close because, in most cases, brokers get a bonus for each day you close early.

This is just one way to locate good deals. Again, I suggest that you keep five or six methods working constantly. Don't rely on just one.

OUT-OF-STATE OWNERS

A good source of motivated sellers is out-of-state landholders. It is difficult for most people to manage a property from a great distance. Even the smallest problems appear large in the mind of a person who is not on the scene.

If a property is vacant, usually no one is available to pick up papers, mow the grass, and make the house appear inhabited.

As a result, many owners worry, justifiably, about vandalism, theft, insurance cancellation, weather damage to the property, etc. All this can work to your advantage when negotiating a good deal.

If the property is rented, a host of other problems for the owner comes to mind. Collection of late rents, eviction proceedings, maintenance work demanded by tenants, finding and screening new tenants, and generally just keeping track of the property can all be big worries for the out-of-state owner. Many owners don't trust management companies or believe they can afford one, but they feel they can't handle their affairs alone, either. Send letters to all of them, offering to take away those concerns. You'll find that some of those owners are highly motivated.

A list of out-of-state owners can be obtained from a list service that has downloaded the tax rolls into its computer. Sometimes REALTORS® can generate the names from their MLS service. It may take a bit of a search to find someone who can supply the names, but when you find that person, the results are well worth the effort. Remember, in most cases, no one else knows the house is for sale. In fact, quite often even the seller doesn't know it until your letter plants the seed in his or her mind.

> *I once met a gentleman who had computerized the names of all the out-of-town owners of property in my area. He gave me permission to search for names based on whatever criteria I wanted. I had him pull up the names of all the out-of-town owners of single-family homes, within a certain range of assessed value, in the Jacksonville area. I ended up with a list of 4,445 names.*
>
> *I then wrote a one-page letter and sent it to 500 of those names to see what would happen. It was a simple letter that basically said, "I buy houses in your area, and I noticed that you are from out of town. Would you be interested in selling?" I put a little reply card on the bottom so they could easily let me*

know they were interested. (See Appendix D for a sample letter to mail to absentee owners.)

Of the 500 letters I sent, I got 10 replies; of the 10 replies, I ended up buying one house. One owner wrote back and said she wanted $8,000 for her house. On further investigation, I discovered that she had not even seen the house in 22 years! She had placed it in the hands of a local management company, who had rented it to a tenant who was paying only $150 a month in a market where $400 had been the customary rent for many years.

The house was a concrete block building with a new roof, and it was in fairly good condition. I knew immediately that the property was worth $35,000, which was the low end of the market. I interviewed the tenant, and found that she had been living there a long time and would love to own the house.

To make a long story short, I accepted the owner's offer at once. I sent her a contract and asked her to sign and return it. I took the signed contract to the title company, which then sent a deed, also to be signed, with instructions.

To deliver the money, I obtained a first mortgage loan from a private lender for $17,000 (the owner possessed the house free and clear). The lender didn't even ask for an appraisal. He just looked at the property. The terms of the loan were 18% interest for seven years, with payments of $350 a month.

Why did I go to a private lender with a high interest rate? I didn't want to be personally liable for the loan. It was a corporate loan, and I obtained it as a corporate officer. Also, I didn't want to have to qualify to anybody, and I didn't want such a loan on my credit report. I've designed my life so that I don't have to qualify to anybody for anything. That's one of the things I teach in my courses.

After paying $8,000 for the house and more than $1,500 for closing costs, which were high because it *was a private loan and I had used a mortgage broker, I had about $7,500 left. At that point, I visited the tenant and said, "Mary Ellen, would you like to own this house?"*

She said, "Mr. LeGrand, I don't have any money to put down on it."

So I said, "What if you not only didn't need any money to put down on it, but if I did these little repairs that need to be done? Would you like to own the house then?"

To which she replied, "Mr. LeGrand, I would love to own this home! I think God sent you!"

Who knows. Maybe he did.

I then explained that the rent she had been paying for years was way below what it should have been. She admitted that this was true. So I made the following deal with her: I immediately raised the rent to $350 per month, which she could afford, and told her that if she paid me $350 a month on time for a year, I would sell her the house for $35,000 with no down payment. I also told her we would work out the terms of the 30-year mortgage payments for the entire term of the loan.

What I did here was create a mortgage on which I would receive $350 a month for 30 years. The cash flow was structured to be a wash during the early years when I would be making loan payments on the seven-year note. But it is obvious that, after I pay off that mortgage, I will continue to receive $350 each month for 23 years thereafter. That's a total of $96,000 in profit.

The only problem was the fact that Mary Ellen was 68 years old when I made the deal with her. I tied up this loose end by having her buy a mortgage life insurance policy naming me as the beneficiary. This policy will pay me the balance of the $35,000 if she passes away before paying off the mortgage note.

It should be noted that I could have dislodged this lady from the rental home, done a little work on it, retailed it for $35,000 cash to an FHA or VA buyer, and walked away with a lot of cash almost immediately. Why didn't I do that? The fact is that the lady deserved to live in that house. She had already paid for it by living in it for 22 years. She just didn't own it yet. So I chose to leave her there instead of booting her out. As it turned out, I received a payday up front, and I'll get another payday in the future.

While this was a good money maker, it certainly wasn't one of my most profitable deals. But I think of it as one of my best deals because it helped an tenant finally realize the American Dream of home ownership. That has to have something to do with it.

DEFAULTED PAPER

Previously, we've discussed several ways to locate bargains in single-family houses. This section is devoted to a little-known, rarely used technique called "buying defaulted paper."

Every house that carries a mortgage or trust deed is a candidate. And the process is a simple one of seeking out loans that are in foreclosure, or about to be in foreclosure, and buying the paper instead of the property.

You are probably thinking that your biggest fear from taking back a mortgage has always been having to foreclose if the payments aren't made. And now I'm suggesting that you actually go looking for paper in default?

YOU BET I AM!

You are looking for defaulted paper so you can buy it at a deep discount and get into the property through the back door. Once you own the mortgage, you have several choices.

First, you can foreclose and own the house. **Second**, you can renegotiate the note and help the owner avoid foreclosure by adding the back payments to the note. **Third**, you can give the owner a little cash for a deed, thus letting him avoid foreclosure.

Let's take a look at the second option. What if we cured the foreclosure by restructuring the note, setting up a new payment based on the increased amount from adding all the back due interest to the principal and then selling the note for a quick profit?

Of course, this will only work in those cases where the owner wants to restructure, and where a temporary problem existed that put him or her in arrears. In cases where restructuring won't work, your objective is to take title to the property as fast and as inexpensively as possible.

> *Recently, I purchased two second mortgages from a bank. Those mortgages were behind FHA firsts in foreclosure.*
>
> *The first deal involved a $50,000 house with a $10,800 first which was $2,000 behind. The face amount of the second mortgage I purchased was $15,000; it was $1,600 behind in payments, leaving a $16,600 payoff. The bank contacted me and offered to sell me the note for $10,000, so it could get out without foreclosing. After some legwork, I went back to the bank with a $5,000 offer, and we settled on $6,000.*
>
> *The first thing I tried to do was get the two loans refinanced for the owners. Had I succeeded, I would have received my $16,600 for a nice $10,600 profit. If this failed, I would then try to buy out the owners for a couple of thousand and resell the house for $50,000, making a nice $25,000 profit. If they wouldn't sell, I'd foreclose and sell the houses four or five months later for a hefty profit.*
>
> *Another alternative would have been for me to make up the first, restructure the second, and let the owners start over again. That would mean I'd have $8,000 cash in this deal, so I'd have to just sit on it and receive a tremendous yield on my $8,000, or sell the note for a profit. This is assuming, however, that I would want the current owner to remain in the house.*

Let me tell you what actually happened on this transaction, since it's now completed.

First, it might be noteworthy to mention that I didn't have a dime in this. I let a friend who had been bugging me for a deal put up all the money. We tried to get the owners refinanced, but their credit was so bad and their balance so high, it wasn't possible.

Finally, we gave up on getting them a loan and tried to buy the house from them. We offered $3,000 net to them and a free month's rent. They refused the offer because they were convinced that some miracle would solve all their problems before they could be put out. This left us with no choice but to foreclose, and that's exactly what we did.

On the day of the sale at the courthouse steps, the owners filed bankruptcy to stop the proceedings. Since they had filed Chapter 13 for reorganization, the judge ordered them to start making payments within 30 days. Arrangements also were made for them to start paying on the arrearages, as well.

Thirty days passed and still no payment was received, so we reinstituted the foreclosure process. Once again we got right up to the sale — and they converted from Chapter 13 to Chapter 7 (total liquidation). This again stopped the sale, but not for very long. Our attorney petitioned the court to continue the sale, and the process resumed. About 45 days later, we owned the house. The owners had run out of tricks.

Look at the following recap of the numbers, so you can see why we got involved in the first place. By the way, the whole process took only 12 months from the time we bought the note until we sold the house. After you look at the numbers, you decide whether the deal was worth the effort.

Note that the items marked with an * were the only ones requiring a cash outlay. The rest were deducted from the sales proceeds. Therefore, my investor paid only $17,500 in cash to get an $8,250 (50% profit) return on his money in one year. Incidentally, that is much longer than it usually takes.

Note purchase price	$ 6,000*
1st mortgage balance	10,800
Cost to bring 1st current	2,000*
Attorney fees to foreclose	1,500*
Holding costs	2,000*
Repair costs	6,000*
Sales costs (including realtor)	$ 4,200
TOTAL COSTS	$ 32,500
Sales Price	$ 49,000
NET PROFIT	**$ 16,500**

That's a 50% return on investment. Probably just a little higher than the return on my investor's CD at the bank. On the other hand, what was my return? It's called infinite! You can't measure it because I had no investment. Whichever way the deal goes, I always win.

The second note I bought involved a similar deal. It was a $6,000 second behind an FHA first of $22,800 on a $50,000 house. That house needed about $3,000 in work, and both mortgages were about 10 months behind. Since the loan-to-value (LTV) ratio was much higher on this property, I wasn't very motivated to buy when the bank said it wanted $1,500 for the note. But when I offered the bank $300 and it accepted, I just couldn't resist. I figured, for $300, what the heck, go for it. My options were the same as those that applied to the other house. In this case, however, I was a lot more motivated to restructure and just receive payments because I was leaving only $300 on the table rather than $8,000. (In the first deal, I had promised my partner a cash profit, so we had to liquidate.)

In the second case, however, I visited the owner, who was a single lady, and discovered that she had made her first mortgage current a few days earlier, thus stopping the foreclosure process. The bank hadn't bothered to check the status of the first before selling the note to me.

This left me in a good position to try to solve the seller's problem, with no further cash outlay, while still making a profit for myself. I discovered she really wanted to keep her house, so I simply offered to add her arrearage to the principal amount she owed, leave her payments the same, and turn the situation into a monthly cash flow. She loved the idea, so I had her sign a mortgage modification to effect the changes.

To this day, she is paying me $149 per month. So far, I've collected 24 payments and still have about 85 more due. I wonder what kind of yield I'm getting, collecting $149 per month on my $300 investment for seven years? I'll leave that up to you computer whizzes to calculate while I'm out looking for some more defaulted paper.

The second deal worked out a lot more easily than the first one. Not bad for a $300 investment. There's gold in defaulted paper, once you learn a few simple rules and how to put them to use.

REALTORS®

Get to know two or three REALTORS® with whom you can work. They have access to hundreds of houses for sale, plus all the necessary information. Once they learn what you're looking for, they'll send you so much information that all you have to do is simply sift through it and pick out the properties on which you wish to make offers. Having all the facts saves everyone a lot of running around. Sometimes REALTORS® will also know the seller's motivation; this can be very valuable to you when you're making an offer.

If you expect to stay on good terms and develop a relationship with a REALTOR®, make sure you inspect the property and can live with your offer before you make it. Act like a professional and the real estate professionals will be at your beck and call. Act like a time waster and you'll soon be on your own.

Be sure to seek out those REALTORS® who deal in bank repos, also. Some of the best deals you will ever make are going to be bank repos. The sellers are motivated and unemotional, and they almost always list with a broker when ready to sell.

REALTORS® are always an excellent source of killer deals. The wise use of a good agent can greatly enhance the number of bargains you find. In fact, if you're busy making a living in another business or job, this could possibly be the only source you need to supply more houses than you can handle.

Most real estate offices that subscribe to the Multiple Listing Service (MLS) have a computer with enough information in it to keep an agent working full-time just finding bargains for you. That computer places a smorgasbord of information right at your fingertips. It contains most of the houses listed in your area and enough information for you to formulate offers.

Just think! Instead of getting on the phone, researching each house, and collecting facts from sellers, you can turn on a machine and get 80% of what you need to know just by punching a button. These listings contain the location, size, construction, mortgage data, amenities, asking price, seller motivation, property condition, and much more information that may be helpful. You can usually even search out vacant houses. Do you think owners of vacant houses are motivated? You bet they are!

What if you make an appointment with a REALTOR® and, together, you sit down at the computer and spend an hour searching for prospects that meet your criteria? Your goal is to end up with 20 prospects that would appear to have motivated sellers. You could, for example, stipulate that you want to know about houses that need repairs. That sort of information usually shows up in the comments section of listings.

Key words that might catch your attention include "handyman special," "as is," "no warranties," "needs work," "investor special," "needs TLC," "estate sale," "foreclosure," and "bank owned."

It's time-consuming to search through these listings to pick out the pearls, but it's to your benefit to do it or have it done while you're in the REALTOR'S® office, instead of wasting time looking at dead ends.

Here's a suggestion that will let you cut to the chase much more quickly. Look only for houses that need work that are listed well below the after-repair value. That way, when you make a low offer on a house that's already listed low, there won't be such a big spread between the asking price and your offer.

Sometimes lenders will list a house at retail, after-repaired price, even though it needs $10,000 of work. They know they won't get the asking price. Your submitting a sensible offer well below their asking price creates sticker shock, and the large reduction is just too much for them to overcome. Quite often the person responsible for accepting the offer doesn't even know the condition of the house.

If your REALTOR® doesn't use a computer, he or she will probably use the MLS books which contain the same information. The only difference is that you have to browse through the books to find the motivated sellers, rather than have the computer spit them out for you. When I started in this business, I used the MLS book to buy my first 23 houses. Either way will work if you know what you're looking for.

After you have spent one hour with the REALTOR®, you should have 10 to 20 properties to evaluate. Of course, all these prospects show signs of motivation, which is a key ingredient. Your next move is to inspect all 20 houses. You need to see their condition and the area, to get a good idea of the value after repairs, assuming the houses need work. Remember, most of these houses are vacant, if that was one of the criteria you put in the computer.

Usually, you will be able to look in the windows and see 80% of the house. This will give you a good idea of the condition and layout, so you can make an intelligent offer. There is no need to run a REALTOR® ragged showing vacant houses. You can inspect the interior after the seller has shown some interest in your offer. This will save countless hours of your REALTOR'S® time and make him or her more willing to work with you.

With this information in hand, combined with the ability to construct offers, you can now go back to your REALTOR® and make an offer on every house you looked at. I'm not suggesting that the REALTOR® physically write up each offer and submit it. Simply get him or her to call the listing agents to submit your offer orally. If there is any interest on the other end, your REALTOR® will be asked to submit your offer in writing. Again, calling first saves a lot of time and effort for REALTORS® and allows them to submit more offers.

I know! You're saying the REALTORS® will steal the deals from you if there is nothing in writing. Don't sweat it. It just isn't so. If they are licensed and this happens, they won't be licensed long. REALTORS® live by a strict code of ethics, and they are governed closely by the state. They must disclose everything and bear heavy responsibility for their actions. You should be more concerned about finding REALTORS® with positive attitudes than worrying about having a deal stolen from you. Besides, most REALTORS® are so busy making a living they don't have time to make any money. They're only looking for a commission check.

Think about what's been done. You've spent one hour collecting prospects, two hours looking at houses, and one hour getting the offers back to your REALTOR®. Now it's in his or her hands to finish the deal. While you're working or playing, the REALTOR®is submitting your offers and getting either a yes, a no, or a counteroffer.

Let's look at the advantages of using a REALTOR®:
- Someone else is doing most of the work.
- You never deal directly with a seller.
- You are multiplying your efforts.
- Your time is free to do other things.
- You won't have to face rejections.
- Your seller cannot voice objections to you, or try to bump up your offer. He must go through a counteroffer procedure.
- Your liability is reduced because a REALTOR® is involved.
- You saved countless hours not chasing dead ends.

One word of caution, however. A REALTOR® is not obligated to give you any information from the MLS. In fact, in most areas, it is against MLS policy for the public to have access to the system. It is a privilege paid for by REALTORS® to be used only by REALTORS®. However, most agents will cooperate and give you the information in an effort to make sales, especially if you convince them you are a serious buyer and aren't there to waste their time.

Last month with the help of a REALTOR®, I put six houses under contract to purchase. Four of them were listed. REALTORS® have always been an excellent source of good deals for me, as well as a big help taking care of details. In return, they get their commissions, the seller makes a sale, the MLS collects a fee, the closing agent writes title insurance, the termite man gets a check, a lender ultimately makes a loan, a hazard insurance premium is generated, and a repair crew gets to work. Everybody wins!

Make friends with some REALTORS® in your area. They can play a valuable role in your success. Develop a good working relationship, and it may turn into a lifelong friendship.

If you hold a license yourself and you're working with other REALTORS®, I suggest you let them have the total commission on your purchase, unless you're dealing in high-value areas where there is a big enough check to go around. Remember, a REALTOR® closing a sale at 6 1/2% commission on a $25,000 purchase is only receiving $1,625 total commission.

And he might have to split that with his broker or other agents. He is not getting rich. Give the REALTOR® the commission while you take the big profit. That's fair isn't it? Don't forget, without the services of that REALTOR®, you won't have a profit because you won't have a deal.

Don't be greedy!

The best place to find a compatible REALTOR® is right in your investment club, if you have one. REALTOR® club members are educated in your ways and speak your language. This will make working with them a lot easier. If you don't have a club in your area, just ask around for a REALTOR® who deals with investors, especially those who handle REO®s.

The first question I would ask a REALTOR® is, "Will you be embarrassed to make low offers?" If the answer is yes, keep looking. You're searching for a professional who is aggressive and serious about getting the job done. He or she must have good follow-up procedures and treat you like the important client you will become. Of course, this should become automatic after you close a couple of deals and prove your value to the REALTOR®.

If you're serious about buying houses and aren't currently working with a good REALTOR®, I suggest that now is the time to find one.

Another good way to generate income and increase your client base is to become a mortgage lender. We'll discuss lending in detail in the next chapter.

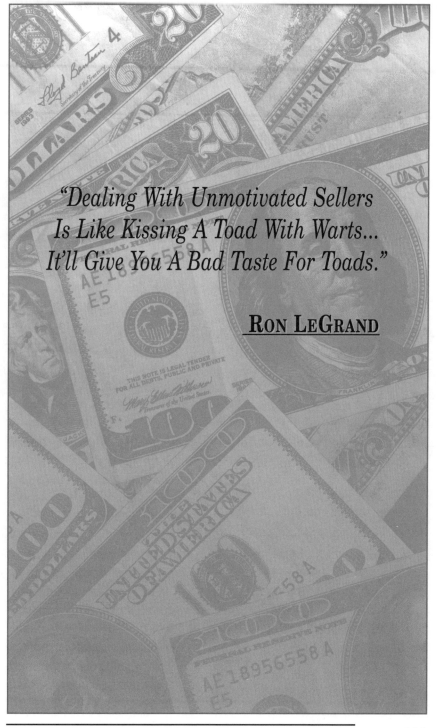

"Dealing With Unmotivated Sellers Is Like Kissing A Toad With Warts... It'll Give You A Bad Taste For Toads."

RON LEGRAND

Many receive advice.
Only the wise profit from it.

Syrus

Chapter

Mortgage Lending

Few people are aware that mortgage lending is an incredible way to build wealth in a hurry. It is an excellent source of leads, as well. It is called the "backdoor" of foreclosure, and many times it can lead you to acquire good properties at deep discounts and receive a fine return on your investment.

Are you getting a 15% or more yield from your CDs, stocks, savings accounts, IRAs, pension plan, and other investments? You should be! You can control your investments and make them grow safely at three to five times your current rate. Yes, I know that sounds too good to be true, but it isn't.

I'm going to share information with you about a technique that is widely used in real estate circles in every city in America. Smart people have been utilizing this investment tool for years. In fact, entire companies have been built around this technique; those who practice it properly have seen tremendous growth in returns. This is a very safe investment that produces high yields while providing security and liquidity.

Do you know what $25,000 is worth in five years compounded at a 7% yield? It's worth $35,000. Now, let's take that same $25,000 and invest it for the same five years at 15% interest instead of 7%. In this case, it has grown to an amazing $52,000! That's a $17,000 difference, simply by increasing the yield from 7% to 15%; and remember, that's in only five years.

If you look at the figures for a 10-year term, your $25,000 would be worth $50,000 at 7%, but if you change the yield to just 15%, the amount grows to an unbelievable $111,000! Folks, that's $61,000 free dollars you will actually receive simply by increasing your yield. Can you really afford not to control your own investments? Does it make sense for a bank to manage your investments for you?

There is an alternative to CDs and mutual funds. It involves private mortgage loans. You can loan money, secured by a first or second mortgage or trust deed, and enjoy not only the safety you want, but also the high yield we've discussed, or more!

PROS AND CONS OF LOANING TO HOMEOWNERS

First, let's clarify the kinds of loans we might make. I'm not talking about the high LTV (Loan To Value) loans the banks and savings and loans make. We're dealing with very low LTV loans. By that, I mean no higher than 50% or 60% of the value of the property securing the loan. This means that, if a house appraises for $60,000, you wouldn't make a loan for more than $36,000. That's a 60% LTV.

It's clear why this approach is safer than that taken by most lending institutions. The banks are in trouble because they make loans at an 80%, 90%, or even 95% LTV ratio. They have no cushion in case of default. Also, when you're dealing with a 60% maximum LTV, there's so much equity above your loan that, should you foreclose, the property could be sold not only for enough to cover your investment, but often at a huge profit.

If you are real estate oriented, this is just another avenue of income for you. And if you are not real estate oriented, there are always scores of investors who would love to have the property for 50% to 60% of the value if you took it back. I am talking a lot about default here, but the reality is that, when a loan is at such a low LTV ratio, default is not common.

Let me answer some of your questions about making loans. Is this a mortgage pool? No! You make the whole loan yourself. You get a lien against the property. You are the bank. You are in total control.

Do I need a lot of cash? No! I've made loans as small as $2,000. The amount of the loan is determined by the borrower's needs.

Who handles all the details? Well, in my opinion, unless you are highly skilled in real estate matters, you should use a good mortgage broker. They will not only find the borrowers for you, but they will also provide proper documentation and protect your interest. All of this costs you nothing. All costs are paid by the borrower. If you make a $10,000 loan, you send a check for $10,000 to the closing agent and you get a mortgage or deed of trust for $10,000.

Do I have to collect payments? Absolutely not! Your mortgage broker will set up your account with a collection agent, if you wish, who will collect each payment when due and deposit it into your account. This can and should be a hassle-free investment. In fact, I strive to keep my investors as far away from collection as possible, for that reason. You may be surprised to know that your bank will even collect the payments for you if you wish.

Is this a long-term investment? No! It can be any term you want. You're the boss. Usually a private investor wants a five-year term or less, but some don't care if it stretches to 10 or 15 years. You can pick a term that suits your strategy for retirement. Some investors make interest-only loans with a short-term balloon; some will amortize for 10 or 15 years and balloon in five; some people prefer the longer term. It's your money, and it's your choice. Of course, the broker is going to come to you with a term that suits the borrower. If that works for you, it's a go. If not, it's up to him to change your mind or to find another investor.

What if I want to liquidate? Mortgages and trust deeds are purchased every day, like stocks. If you want out, it will take from two weeks to a month to sell your note. Since your interest rate will be 15% or higher, you will take very little, if any, discount when you sell. You really shouldn't make mortgage loans if you feel you will liquidate shortly, but the option is always available. Just call your mortgage broker and he or she will handle all the details.

Who borrows at 15%? All kinds of folks! Some have good credit, some have poor credit. Some are owner/occupants, some are investors. These folks have learned that it's not the cost of money that counts, but the availability of it. In the case of an owner/occupant, they may not qualify under bank terms for a variety of reasons, such as poor credit, time on the job, or debt ratio. In many cases, they could qualify but just don't want to deal with the banks. They would rather pay the high rates in exchange for the ease of getting the money. This also holds true for investors. I often have made it possible for investors to acquire good deals in houses because the funds weren't available from banks but were available from private lenders.

If an investor becomes skilled at locating good deals, the purchase price will be well below the after-repair value of the house. The bank, however, wants to loan on the purchase price, not the value of the house, thus penalizing the investor for being astute. Having the money available will make or break the deal. Paying a higher interest rate is irrelevant compared to the loss of thousands of dollars in profit if the money was not available.

Remember, as a lender, you will not lend more than 50% to 60% LTV regardless. You're making a safe loan in either case, whether it be to an investor or to an owner/occupant. You should never make a loan without a 40% to 50% safety net. If you don't violate that rule, you should always come out a winner.

What are my options if my borrower doesn't pay? Actually, there are several options in the event of default by your borrower. Foreclosure is only one of those options, and it is usually last on the list.

The first thing you can do, if your borrower's problem is temporary, is restructure the note. For example, let's say your borrower has been out of work for three months and is two months behind on his payments to you. Now he finds a new job and would like to keep this house, but he can't come up with enough money to bring you current in one lump sum. You could let him continue to make regular payments and make an extra payment on his arrearage, or you could simply add the arrearage to the principal balance and extend the term of the loan. This means you would be collecting interest on interest for the entire remainder of the loan. There is almost always a way to work out a payment problem, if both sides are willing.

Incidentally, when this happens, some of my lenders will charge a reinstatement fee as well as the back payments. Remember, it's up to you to decide whether your borrower can reinstate or not. Once a loan is in default, you have the right to call it due or allow reinstatement. It's your choice. You don't have to take the payments unless you want to. Therefore, you are well within your rights to pick up an extra $100, $200, or $300 to allow reinstatement. This is especially true if you elect to add the fee to the loan and don't force the borrower to pay it in cash. That, of course, is also your option. At this point, you are in total control.

Certainly, you would only allow a reinstatement if the borrower has solved his problem and can continue to make payments. In any case, you have other options.

You can offer to buy the house from your borrower in lieu of foreclosure. This is an opportunity for you to get a house at a greatly discounted price and avoid foreclosure at the same time. Your borrower has the option of either taking some money now and selling you the house, or being foreclosed and getting nothing. When this happens, you have created a tremendous profit center by reselling the house.

Some investors make private loans in the hope that this will happen; others would rather not get involved with the real estate at all. Either way you win. As I said earlier, when you can sell a house at 50% to 70% of its value, there are scores of investors who would take it off your hands. In fact, there are businesses built around tracking down these kinds of deals.

If you have an uncooperative borrower and you can't restructure, then you are left with either selling your note or foreclosing.

Yes, there are investors who are willing to buy your note, even if it's in default. In fact, that's the way they want it! They can either force payment of debt or get the house. However, if you sell a note in default, you usually will have to discount it, so this isn't my favorite option.

If I am left with no other choice, I simply foreclose. Foreclosure isn't the evil, time-consuming, costly, legal process that most people think it is. It's as simple as sending your note to an attorney and saying, "Do it." Then all you have to do is sit back and wait. Nine times out of 10, before foreclosure is complete, someone will be calling your attorney's office requesting a payoff letter. Your loan will get paid off. When this happens, you will collect all accrued interest, your principal balance, and all attorney's fees, court costs, and all other expenses you have incurred in connection with your loan.

You see, when you're into a property at 50% or less, there are always lenders who are willing to refinance, relatives who will bail them out, or scores of buyers who will buy them out.

If none of this happens, you will get the house; then, you will have the options we discussed earlier.

What if my borrower files for bankruptcy? You have a lien against the house. You cannot be wiped out by bankruptcy. If your borrower files Chapter 7, you should be able to continue with the foreclosure process. It will be slowed, but it won't be stopped. You have a secured debt and a right to seize the asset.

If Chapter 13 for reorganization is filed, your borrower will be ordered to continue with his monthly payments and probably an additional payment on his arrearage. In the event that one payment is missed, you then can proceed with the foreclosure process and, usually, within 30 to 60 days, the process will be complete. Bankruptcy will slow the procedure, but it won't keep you from collecting your debt.

What happens if I take a second and the first doesn't get paid? If you are in second position and you aren't getting paid, chances are that the first is also in arrears. In that case, to protect your interests, you would simply bring the first current while starting collection action on your second. In most states, you must be notified of any foreclosure action by the first.

You'll have plenty of time to react. Remember, you are entitled to collect any money you have advanced. That includes any payments you've made on the first. Part of your closing package, if you're loaning on a second, is mortgage verification on the first. This will include all the loan information and the loan's current status.

Frequently, small seconds are made to people who are in foreclosure for just enough to bring their loan current.

Obviously, such a loan stands a much higher chance of going into default. If you're an investor who is not real estate oriented or one who would really rather not own the property, then you wouldn't want this kind of loan. On the other hand, if you see owning the property as a larger profit producer, you might consider specializing in foreclosure loans.

Many investors tend to forget that just because you wind up with the house, you don't have to keep it. It can be sold immediately at a wholesale price, producing a profit over and above the already high yield on your loan. There is no law that says you have to be a landlord and deal with tenants just because you own the house.

Of course, some people will say that you are taking advantage of people in trouble. If that's how you feel, then don't make loans to people in foreclosure. Let them stay in foreclosure and lose their home. Heaven forbid we should ever be accused of taking advantage.

Just remember, they were in foreclosure long before you came along. You had nothing to do with that. Also remember that you are probably their only hope of saving their home. When you bail them out of a foreclosure, they agree to make payments to you on the money you loaned them. If they do, you've supplied them with a valuable service they won't get anywhere else. If they don't pay, are they any worse off than they were before you made them the loan? You decide.

If you are going to make loans to people in foreclosure, let's not forget the basics. The loans must still be low LTV with plenty of equity cushion in case of default. Common sense still prevails.

On the other hand, it doesn't hurt to be a little creative sometimes. For example, what if someone comes along with a house worth $70,000, he owes $50,000 on the first, and he needs $4,000 to stop foreclosure? Under normal circumstances, you wouldn't make the loan because the LTV greatly exceeds the 50% to 60% ceiling. But let's suppose this family has another house with a lot of equity they could use as collateral; or maybe Mom and Dad are willing to offer their house as collateral. This would put you in a very secure position and ensure your repayment. It's as simple as getting enough collateral, so you feel comfortable you will collect one way or the other. It's a matter of whichever way you win first.

What kind of documents should you receive? Your closing package should contain the following:

1. An original note.

2. A copy of the mortgage or trust deed. The original will be recorded and then sent to you.

3. A fire insurance endorsement naming you as mortgagee.

4. An assignment of rents allowing you to collect rents in case of default.

These documents should be drawn up even if the house is owner occupied. If the owner moves out and rents, you don't want him collecting rents while you are foreclosing. This document gives you the right to start collecting immediately upon default.

5. A first mortgage verification (if you're making a second).

6. An application filled out by your borrower.

7. A title insurance policy for the amount of your loan insuring you against any title defects.

8. A recent appraisal of the property.

9. Some lenders like to have a termite report, as well, to ensure there is neither serious damage under the house nor live infestation. If damage exists, money could be put in escrow for the repairs and released to the contractors on completion.

Are there other avenues of income from loans? Yes, there are. We've talked about reinstatement fees and making money with the property if you get it back. Now, let's discuss some other goodies that occur when the loans are repaid as agreed, which is most of the time.

One of those is transfer fees. Some investors get a $100 to $300 transfer fee if the house is sold and someone else assumes the loan. If you put a due-on-sale clause in your loan, you are in total control upon transfer. The borrower pays the fee or you can call the loan due.

Another nice income can be made from prepayment penalties. These are penalties incurred when a loan is paid off early. It's a technique commonly used by finance companies and small lending institutions to create another profit center. The penalty can be a percentage of the unpaid balance, or several months' interest on the unpaid balance.

For example, the note could be worded in such a way that, if it's paid off before it's due, you would receive three months' interest in addition to the regular interest. Folks, this can amount to a lot of money for a lender, because those loans are almost always paid off before they expire. If you are receiving a three-month interest penalty on a $20,000 loan at 15% interest, you're getting an extra $750 over and above what you're owed. Yes, this is legal; and no it's not usury in most states. Check with your attorney or mortgage broker to make sure you don't cross the line on prepayment penalties.

Late penalties also increase your yield. All loans should contain a late penalty. My late penalty is 10% after five days. This means that, if the $200 payment isn't received by the 5th of the month, the borrower must pay an additional $20.

Can the mortgage broker run off with my money? The broker should never be in possession of your money. Make your check out directly to the closing agent for the gross amount of the loan. The closing agent will then cut a check to the broker. Remember, you aren't paying the broker; the borrower is. You should have no expenses. Your payments should be collected by your bank or a collection company. In short, if your broker never has your money, he can't run off with it.

Is my investment really as safe as it sounds? Yes! As long as you've followed the guidelines that we've discussed and apply common sense. No, mortgages aren't as hands-off as mutual funds or stocks or other kinds of non-participation investments. But, in return for a little effort on your part, your money will grow two, three, or even four times faster than your current investments, and you maintain control. If you follow some simple guidelines when making loans, your risk will be minimal. **Briefly, these guidelines are:**

- **Make only low LTV loans . . . no exceptions! An appraisal will confirm the value.**
- **Get title insurance for the amount of your loan.**
- **Have professionals close the loan.**
- **Make sure fire insurance is maintained on the property at all times.**
- **Take action immediately in case of default.**

Remember, making loans is a business and should be treated like a business.

If you set up a simple system and let the professionals implement that system, your loan portfolio can be hassle-free and produce staggering yields. And remember, all costs are to be paid by the borrower . . . not you!

USING YOUR OWN PENSION PLAN

How do I use my IRAs or pension plan? Making real estate loans is an approved and widely-accepted use for IRAs and pension plans. Think of it! Now, you can not only loan money that has been unavailable for you to use, but you can also make it grow rapidly, tax deferred! Since Uncle Sam isn't taking a bite out of your profits until you draw out the money, more money is left in the account to compound and grow. The results are staggering. You'll be receiving interest on interest on interest, and it's all legal and approved by the IRS.

If you are to use retirement accounts for loans, they must be administered by a Third Party Administrator, or TPA. This TPA is set up and approved to administer your loan activities. This means you will probably have to transfer your plan to one of these TPAs unless, of course, your present administrator is set up to do that. But the likelihood of that happening is slim to none.

When your TPA is located, simply send the transfer form to them and they'll do all the work for you. Once you've done that . . . you're ready to make loans!

When you've located a loan, you simply let your TPA know where to send the check for the gross amount of the loan, and you're in business. There should be no cost to you except your plan administration costs. Your setup fee, for collecting the monthly payments from your borrower, can be collected at closing from the loan proceeds, if you instruct your broker or closing agent to do so. Some TPAs will even collect the monthly payments for you and deposit them into your account.

There are some restrictions when dealing with IRAs, such as provisions against self-dealing, but your TPA will furnish you with all the facts on request.

We've covered a lot of information in just a few pages. I hope I've enlightened you on the awesome power of making real estate loans. If the concept appeals to you, I can't think of a better time to get started than right now. While most people are complaining about the low rates they're getting on their CDs and other investments, you could be receiving a bare minimum return of 15% all the time — not just when you get a hot stock.

What's it going to be? Are you going to continue to let other people control your money so you can get a return that barely keeps up with inflation? Or are you going to take control and make sure that, when you are ready to retire, you can do everything you want to do — without worrying about money?

LOAN BROKERING

I make a large portion of my income by loaning out other peoples' money. I collect a fee equal to about 10% of the loan and never have to get an OK from a bank. I have hundreds of students nationwide who have discovered this business and turned it into a full-time career. It's an easy business with huge rewards, and it works in all 50 states.

To learn more about private lending and/or becoming a mortgage broker, so you can make huge fees loaning money from other private lenders, you should know about **The Money Tree**, a course I have designed. Its purpose is threefold:

First, it teaches private investors why they should be making mortgage or deed of trust loans for huge yields. **Second**, it shows Quick-Turn house investors how to tap the lender market to get all the money they need to buy the good deals without going to a bank and without qualifying. **Third**, it completely covers the business of being a mortgage broker in any state.

The Money Tree course contains six audiocassette tapes with a complete workbook, software, and a brochure with an accompanying tape that you can hand to a potential private lender to convince him for you. Simply loan out the tape and follow up. I've made it easy to tap the big bucks.

> *I met a fellow named Khalel Gorgi in one of our boot camps in Atlanta. He had bought my course a few months earlier when I spoke in Atlanta and, fortunately, he decided to do something with it. He found a bank repo worth well over $200,000 repaired situated on four acres. He got a contract accepted — $120,000 all cash.*
>
> *He didn't have that kind of money in his account, so he was faced with a minor problem. Where to get the money? Now, Khalel is from Iran and I suspect they forgot to teach him, when he was growing up, that he couldn't buy things without money. What he did was line up a loan from a private lender for $160,000 at 18% interest. This loan was based on the equity in the house, not his personal qualifications.*
>
> *Khalel spent $20,000 in repair costs and $20,000 in other costs before he sold the house and one of the four acres for $230,000. He gave the buyer an option to buy the other three acres for $75,000 cash, which the buyer claims will close within six months. He will net $130,000 on this one house before he's through with the deal. I don't know about you, but I think*

18% is a lot to pay on his loan. I think he should have passed up this deal and looked for cheaper money, don't you agree? After all, who in his right mind would pay 18% on a loan for six months, just so they could make a measly $130,000 profit?

The answer is me, of course, and you, if you need to. By the way, when we were in Atlanta, Khalel harassed us until we went with him to his favorite Persian restaurant. We really didn't want to go. All I could think about was the last time I had Indian food in Albany, New York, with Paul Bauer and Danny Santucci. I figured Persian food and Indian food were a lot alike and I hate Indian food. As it turned out, it was not only the best food I've had in a long time, but for weeks after I dreamed about returning for more. Khalel doesn't know it yet, but when I return to Atlanta, he's going to take me out for some more fine eating; that is, if he's got time between deals.

Section IV
Savvy Dealing

All people are self made.
Only successful people admit it.

Dan Peña

Chapter

Negotiating Win-Win Deals

Most deals work out differently than the way they are initially presented. We have to make a deal work successfully using the knowledge we have. Negotiate with the seller in such a way that both of you leave with a good feeling whether you make the deal or not. Always remember to negotiate from a position of strength.

UNDERSTANDING THE SELLER'S MOTIVATION

Ascertain the seller's needs and try to fill them. If he or she needs $5,000 cash and you can't get it for them, it doesn't matter how much talking you do. You won't make the deal work.

Listen between the lines. Many times motivation to sell has nothing to do with money. For example, intangibles such as unhappy memories associated with the house, or a long-standing argument with relatives, can cause a person to want to sell fast. Many such reasons will seem irrational to you.

If you listen well, however, you often can meet the seller's needs without cash. A seller may want to leave town by the 26th of the month, and that deadline is more important than the price. If that's the case, then match that requirement with his lowering the price, dropping the interest rate, or making some other concession. Learn the seller's problems and try to solve them.

Remember that one of the seller's understandable, basic needs is to feel safe about your contract offer. Try to use as few contingency clauses as possible. In fact, try to avoid having any. The more contingencies in a contract, the less chance the seller will sign.

THE VIRTUES OF PATIENCE

What do you say to the seller when your gut tells you you have a potentially great deal, but you just don't know how to put it together? One good reply is, "I will work on a way to make it work for both of us and call you back tomorrow."

This is a good line to use if you don't have all the answers and need time to figure out how to make the deal work. Don't be hurried into making an offer you will regret later.

You may be rushed at times, but never make an offer before you find out what the seller wants. This goes for property or anything else. Once you know the seller's needs, make one or more offers at the same time. All these offers are made with the seller's needs in mind, while any one of them will satisfy your own needs.

Always leave the door open if the seller doesn't accept your first offer. Quite often he or she will take less than you were willing to offer in the first place. Some deals age like fine wine, so be patient and work other deals while waiting for a seller to accept.

USING LIENS AND JUDGMENTS IN NEGOTIATIONS

Look for liens on properties. This motivates a seller. Almost any seller who has a lien on his house expects to pay the full amount of the lien when selling. Yet, you can negotiate a deal for half the amount or less with the lien holder to whom the money is owed. Then you can reduce your purchase price by the amount you discounted the liens.

Judgments seldom accrue interest, and, more often than not, they don't attach to the property. If I go to court and get a judgment against someone, the judge hands the judgment to me, and the judgment is recorded at the courthouse. But the judgment may not attach to the property unless I physically get a recorded copy of that judgment and re-record it. This is called "certifying the judgment." Not many people know this, including most attorneys. Just because a judgment is on file doesn't mean that it is attached to the property. Check the law in your area. You should also check to see if it is a verified or certified judgment.

There are several ways to remove a judgment:

- **Negotiate with the holder of the judgment to remove it from the property for a small fee. This will not pay off the judgment, but it will remove it from the property, which is probably all you're trying to accomplish.**

- **Foreclose it off.**

- **Discount it and pay it off.**

Speaking of Interest

Is it possible to obtain a 0% interest loan? Yes, if you are dealing with motivated sellers. You may negotiate one from a seller by just never bringing up the subject of interest. Just offer to pay a certain amount until the debt is paid off.

For example, suppose a seller has a vacant house which no one has come to see. The seller doesn't want it. You drop by with a solution to his problem. You give the seller most of his asking price, plus a small cash down payment of $4,000, on the condition that he carry a mortgage on this free-and-clear house. You approach the seller and say, "I can give you $4,000 down if you will carry the balance for $125 a month until it's paid. Is that all right?"

If the seller asks for interest you say, "Why do you need interest? You have equity in the house and are not getting any interest on it now. I can only afford to give you $4,000 down and $125 a month to make this deal work for me. I have to make repairs and try to market the house myself. This is all this house will support. It is the only way I can buy it. If this works for you, fine; if it doesn't, that's OK. I don't want to make you angry, I just want to make a deal that works for both of us."

You imply that, if he doesn't like it, you will walk out on the deal. If you don't mention interest, the seller probably will not mention it either. Show the seller that the deal depends on the house, not on you.

Remember, however, the real key to getting zero interest loans is to deal with motivated sellers only.

BEING STRAIGHT WITH SELLERS

You don't need to do anything fancy in negotiating. All you have to do is talk to the seller and find out what he or she is trying to accomplish. Be square with them. Tell them honestly what you can do. If it works, fine; if not, that's fine, too. You can't do any more.

If you are resolved that a deal has to meet your conditions or you can't be a part of it, and you relay that idea to the seller in a friendly manner, you don't need to know anything else about negotiation. The negotiation is the easiest part of the process.

Don't waste time with bad leads. If a seller is inflexible, move on to the next lead. If possible, try to negotiate as much as possible over the phone, so that you know if you have the potential for a good deal before you leave your office. I always prequalify a seller thoroughly before I see him or her in person.

Get the facts from the seller; try to fit that information into a deal. Explain exactly what you can do, and why you do what you do. If it doesn't work, move on to the next deal. Don't hide things. Be honest.

I keep thinking of my friend and Boot Camp graduate, Sue Butler from Augusta, Georgia. She called me once to talk and talk and talk about a killer deal she had just closed. That deal had even me green with envy. Sue told me how, in response to her ad, she *had received a call from a seller in foreclosure. He owed $69,000 on a house worth $169,000 in good condition. Sue learned over the phone that the man was several payments behind and willing to walk if someone would pay just a fraction of his equity.*

Sue visited the house and struck up a deal most people wouldn't believe possible. She will retail the house for somewhere near what it's worth, and she'll make an obscene profit. She indicated she would sell half interest in the house to a partner for $25,000 to $35,000 instant cash to her.

She'll let the partner pay the monthly payments while they are selling the house. Then they'll split the profit above her partner's buy-in price, which means Sue makes $25,000 or $35,000 now and half the profit when they sell.

This lady is fired up. She said she is getting more deals than she can possibly handle. I wonder what it would have cost Sue had she chosen not to attend my Boot Camp.

TELL THE SELLER WHY

You can't make the seller's problems your problems, at least not if you plan to stay in this business! If a seller has so much indebtedness on a property that assumption of the payments would lead to negative cash flow, tell him that plainly. If you need for the price to be dropped, say why. If you need more profit in a transaction to make it work, or want to use very little cash to buy your properties, say so. You will make a lot more money by being straightforward about how you do and do not buy property.

There's no big mystery about negotiating. It's as simple as discovering the seller's needs and working out one or more solutions to meet them. If you can't, leave the door open by explaining why you can't. Quite often your professionalism and straightforward approach will lead you right back into the deal at a later date. That's when the seller calls you back because he or she can't get the house sold under their terms or at their price.

Tell it like it is, tell the truth, and back up what you say. If you don't win this one, at least you'll feel good that you did it the right way.

MAKING OBSCENE AMOUNTS OF MONEY WITHOUT EVER TALKING TO A SELLER

If dealing with sellers bothers you and makes you feel inept, there is a good solution to the problem: **DON'T DEAL WITH SELLERS!**

How about taking my suggestion about using a REALTOR®? By utilizing a good agent to help you find the junkers, you can make virtually hundreds of offers on houses and never meet the seller, not even at closing. This is especially true if the seller is a bank or the government. When they sell a house, they just send a package to the closing agent. No one ever appears in person.

So, if dealing with people worries you, and you think it's a good excuse to avoid making offers . . . forget it. I've just destroyed that crutch for you. Time to get to work!

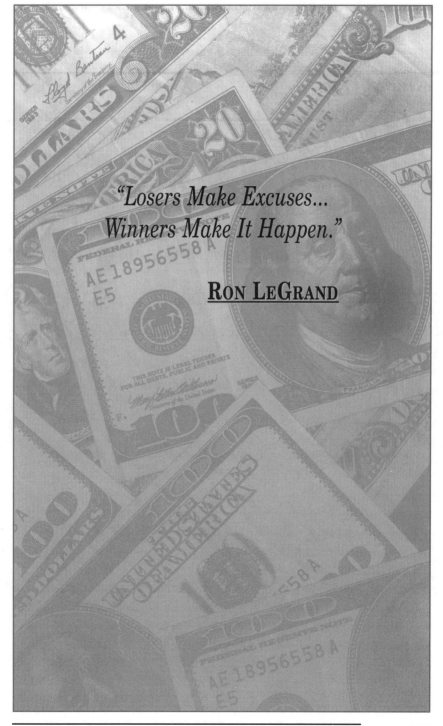

"*Losers Make Excuses...*
Winners Make It Happen."

RON LEGRAND

*History has demonstrated that
the most notable winners usually
encountered heartbreaking obstacles
before they triumphed.
They won because they refused
to become discouraged by their defeats.*

B.C. Forbes

Chapter **12**

Making An Offer
By The Rules

The most important thing to remember about offers is to make them! You can learn how to find motivated sellers, negotiate deals, write contracts, and fix up property; but if you don't use that knowledge, you have wasted your time. Leave behind a trail of offers. Gather facts, then use them to formulate deals. If you don't make offers, you won't buy houses. Unfortunately, too many people become professional information gatherers, then never take the next step.

Until you make an offer and get a response, you will never know just how seriously your seller is motivated. For example, I once found a duplex for which the seller owed $17,000. The house was vacant and needed repairs; there were also two unassumable loans on the property. I discovered it just by driving around and noticing a cheap, ratty "FOR SALE" sign. (That sign indicated that the seller was unsophisticated. Chances are always excellent that you will get a better deal from a FSBO displaying that kind of sign.)

The property was worth $40,000 to $45,000. The seller was asking $25,000 with $8,000 cash to mortgage. I offered $1,000 cash to mortgage, and the seller accepted. The seller didn't even think twice about it! The property was put under contract and sold for $24,000 the next day. If I had not made the offer, it would never have been accepted.

It's easy to offer too much. If you have never tried some really outrageously low offers, make a few just for practice. I once bought a house from a lender for $750 total. The house had a new roof, and it needed no exterior paint and little work on the inside. In jest, I offered $500, and the bank said the minimum it would take was $750. The house appraised for $15,000, as is. It was located in a low-income, high-crime area which made it unattractive to much of the market. I knew, however, that if I bought it cheaply enough, there would be someone who would see it as a good deal regardless of the location. Sure enough, I was right. I sold that house for $5,000 cash.

So, what should you really offer? As a real estate trainer, this is one of the questions I hear most often, and it is not only beginners who ask. Many experienced investors, people who could be expected to know the answer, don't know either. Of course, the definition of "experienced" varies. Having a license and being involved in the real estate industry doesn't qualify anyone to give a definitive answer to "What should I offer?"

The only way to get the correct answer is to learn from someone who really knows. From my years of experience in the business, I have come up with several steps to make this process simple, fast and accurate. Every time I conduct hands-on training in the field, I do the same thing over and over again, no matter what city I'm in or what price range I'm dealing with. My students are shocked to learn how simple it is to make good offers. And it's great to see how fast they catch on after they make a few in real life.

DETERMINING VALUE, THE FOUNDATION OF YOUR OFFER

This section closely parallels the Property Acquisition Worksheet discussed in Chapter 4. It is such a valuable tool for determining a sensible offer that I want you to refer to it as we continue our discussion.

First, you must know the value of the house you're buying. When I say "know the value," I mean the after-repaired, in-excellent-condition, ready-to-sell value. What will be the appraisal value after you've made the house the best looking one in the neighborhood? How much will it sell for compared to other houses that have sold recently in the same area, in similar condition, and with approximately the same amount of square footage?

To find the "comps," or comparables, you must do your homework. Either get a REALTOR® to pull some comps for you or do the research yourself. Don't guess. It's critical for you to determine the real value because everything you do from here on will hinge on that figure.

Some areas have publicly accessible databases of tax rolls and sales. These databases will actually print out a market analysis similar to the MLS service REALTORS® use. If you live in one of those areas, your job will be relatively easy. If not, you must simply do a bit more research prior to making an offer. Please remember that comps come from sales, not asking prices. An easy way to get a REALTOR® to help is to tell him or her that, if you buy the house, you may need his or her services to sell it.

The **second** step is to determine the approximate cost of repairs. This is not as difficult as it sounds. Anyone can do it with a bit of training. I tell my students to separate the work into components, then simply add them up.

For example, a roof on a 1,200-square-foot house will cost $1,500 to $2,000, depending on who does the work. This estimate assumes that you don't use high-priced, union-scale contractors, and that you have shopped a bit before hiring anyone.

Carpet, pad, labor, and linoleum for the same house will cost about $1,000 at $10 per square yard, total price. Interior and exterior painting shouldn't cost more than $1,500. Central heat and air installed shouldn't cost more than $2,500. Window replacement runs anywhere from $75 to $150 per window installed, depending on the size. A complete kitchen can be installed for about $1,000.

I know you're saying that isn't so in your area — that your prices are higher. Well, my friend, it is so in your area when you learn who to hire and what to fix. Just remember, you're not building your dream house here. You're only making your inventory ready to market.

If estimating repair costs is a problem for you, then I suggest that you get help from a friend or a contractor to get a ballpark figure before you make the offer. Or you can attend one of my Boot Camps, where we take you out in the field and work through the estimating process. We cover every aspect of repairs, before and after, and go into great detail on how to estimate costs. Call my office for more information.

A word of caution: Don't spend too much time trying to get an exact repair figure. You're only trying to ballpark it. The objective is to get the offer made, not analyze it to death. A tolerance for mistakes is figured into the formula, as you'll soon see.

To recap, by now you have estimated the sale value of the house and the cost of repairs. (Before you close, get estimates to verify your assumptions.)

The **third** step is to determine your purchase, holding, and sales costs. You can get your purchase costs from any closing agent, REALTOR®, attorney, or experienced investor. Of course, what you negotiate when making an offer will determine what you really pay.

Figure out how long you think it will take to sell the house, and you can get a handle on holding costs. If you think three months, then figure in three or four payments, plus taxes, insurance, and utilities. Be conservative here. A six- or nine-month holding period is not out of the question. Some properties will move fast; others will be on the market for a while. We don't have a crystal ball.

Allow for the worst, but don't go off the deep end. Being too conservative can and will cost you deals because you weren't realistic with your numbers. Sometimes overestimating costs can be worse than underestimating, because it will cause you to make false judgments and lose a deal that could have been a money-maker.

If, for example, you're looking for a $20,000 profit, and your numbers show that if you hold the house for one year instead of six months you'll make only $17,000, is that any reason to kill the deal? Certainly not! It just means you must work harder to sell that house more quickly.

Your sales costs can be figured by first adding projected advertising expenses to commissions paid. Then call the lender you plan to use and ask for an estimated cost of your new loan. Simply quote a sales price and, within seconds, they will tell you your selling costs.

The **fourth** step, and the most fun, is to determine how much profit you want in return for doing all this work. What will it be...$10,000, $20,000, $30,000? You name it — but be realistic. The higher the prices of the properties you're dealing with, the bigger the profit you should seek.

For example, if you're selling a $30,000 house, you're going to have a tough time making a $20,000 profit. On the other hand, in selling a $250,000 house, I would expect a minimum profit of $40,000. Frankly, that's on the low side.

Ron's Rule: The higher the stakes, the bigger the payoff. Remember, your costs are going to add up much more quickly when prices are high. If that's true, then your profit potential should be greater, as well. A good rule of thumb is to plug in a 20% profit of the sales price. But remember, that's only a rule of thumb.

A word of caution! My example of a $150,000 house applies in areas where that amount buys only a bread-and-butter, 1,200-square-foot, three-bedroom house. If your area has decent houses in the $40s, $50s, and $60s, that's where you should deal. Stay where the market is. Don't get "big-deal-itis."

Buying a high-priced house in a low-priced area can lead to gray hairs unless you have the skill and holding power to stay until the house is sold, which may take a while. Remember, we're only talking about buying junkers. If you deal in lease options and assumptions, the sky is the limit after you learn to minimize your risk.

In fact, some of you should specialize in high-priced houses, once you learn the ropes. If you have, or can partner with someone who has the holding power to maintain control, there are huge profits in these houses in today's market. In fact, once you get down to the nitty-gritty and really learn this business, you'll soon discover that it's just as easy to make $50,000 on a house as it is to make $10,000.

Now we're getting to the bottom line. I can sum up everything we've learned so far and put it into one simple equation:

sale price (minus) repair costs (minus) buying, holding, & sales costs (minus) projected profit = maximum allowable offer

After you become familiar with your market and learn how to estimate repairs, the whole process I have just described will take you all of five minutes to complete. Spend that five minutes doing it right, and you might just avoid several months or years correcting your mistake.

Don't be concerned about coming up with the exact numbers when you're trying to evaluate a deal. Your objective is to get within a tolerable range so you can make an offer quickly. If you're in the habit of verifying every figure before you even make an offer, your success rate is going to be very low because you haven't learned to make wise use of your time. Don't get "paralysis of analysis"!

Make the offers, get interest from the buyer, then verify your assumption. If the seller is not going to play ball, why waste time being a number-cruncher on a house you won't buy? So what if you are off $2,000 on your repair estimates! All that means is that you make an $18,000 profit instead of a $20,000 profit. If the $2,000 is that critical, then the deal is too close anyway, and you're offering too much.

Your efforts should be concentrated on making a lot of offers, not collecting facts you won't need on houses you won't buy. If you get carried away with the number-crunching, some other investor will put the property under contract while you're trying to decide what to offer. Believe me! I know this, because I am one of the investors who has taken deals from those who couldn't make a fast decision. You can't Quick-Turn in slow motion!

MAKING THREE OFFERS

It's usually best to make several offers at the same time. This often causes the seller to fix his attention on which offer to accept, rather than on the more logical question of whether any of the offers should be accepted.

Here's an example: 1 was called once about a property with an asking price of $25,000. The property was worth about $47,000 after repairs. I made the following three offers:

First, a cash offer for $15,000.

Second, $4,000 down and $16,000 in six months for a $20,000 purchase price.

Third, $25,000 on sweet terms with the seller taking most of his equity in long-term monthly payments.

The offer for $25,000 was the seller's full price. However, it was on my terms. I offered $3,000 cash down with the seller's carrying a $22,000 mortgage at $150 a month until the balance is paid off, and I made that mortgage subordinate to new financing. It became, in essence, a second mortgage, thus giving me the right to place a new first on the house without paying off the $22,000 mortgage to the seller. (There's more on subordination in Chapter 13.)

Now, the seller had received three offers: one for $15,000 cash; one for $20,000 if he could take a little now and the rest later; and one for full purchase price if he could live with $3,000 now and a payment of $150 a month until the balance was paid.

Probably, it never occurred to him that he didn't have to accept any of those offers. And I didn't care which he accepted. I didn't put the offers in writing. I used a legal pad and wrote the figures on it, then handed it to the seller and asked him which offer he wanted. Only after a seller picks an offer do I write a formal contract.

This is a conversation you might expect.

"Mr. Seller, these are the three ways I can buy your house. See which one suits you and we'll get it working."
"I can't take just $15,000 cash for this house."

The seller will probably need time to think about it. He may want to talk it over with his wife and call you the next morning.

"Mr. Seller, I don't blame you. I wouldn't either."
"I really don't like the idea of collecting payments, because I have no way of knowing that they'll get paid. And I really don't

like the idea of somebody's having a new first mortgage on my property, putting me in second position."

"I don't blame you, Mr. Seller; I wouldn't do it either. I think you ought to take door #2, where you get some down and the balance within a few months.*"*

This is the offer he did take, because his risks were minimal and he saw that he would get all his cash in a short time. However, there is absolutely no way I would know that unless I gave him a choice. I've found that, quite often, the seller takes the offer I least expect.

In this example, the seller was asking $25,000, and the final negotiated price was $20,000 with $4,000 down and $16,000 within six months. There was no interest and no monthly payments. That's what he accepted. I made the three offers mentioned above, and it took him three days to make up his mind.

Within a few days of closing, I sold the property for $27,000. I made $7,000 on this property and the whole process took less than a month. By the way, the seller never even mentioned interest, and neither did I. You see, receiving interest was not important to him. Show me a bank that will allow you to borrow money at no interest!

Interestingly, someone else had offered that seller $22,000 all cash before I came on the scene, but then backed out of the contract because of some termite damage. The cost of repairs was $1,500. I asked the seller to drop the price $1,500, and he did. By the way, the house appraised for $40,000.

In a situation like this, you must know the value before you make an offer. If you don't know the value because you lack experience with that neighborhood or type of property, get help from a REALTOR®, or anyone else who can provide a market analysis.

With a little experience with a certain type of house in a particular area, you will be able to determine the market value when you make your first walk through. Remember, however, when you're in doubt, get help from others who are more experienced.

The exercises at the end of Chapter 13 will give you some practice in forming three offers. Get in the habit of making multiple offers, and you'll see your acceptance rate skyrocket.

ESCAPE CLAUSES

Entire books have been written about escape clauses, sometimes known as "weasel clauses" or "contingency clauses." Such clauses help you void a contract when a deal goes bad. You only need one good one. One example might read, "This contract is contingent on approval of buyer's partner." Your "partner" could be anybody you wish. Another example: "This contract is contingent upon financing acceptable to purchaser." This gives you maximum flexibility either to proceed with the deal, or to end it before closing and have your earnest deposit returned.

While we're on the subject of escape clauses, let me explain what I usually use — NOTHING. That's right, none. I've found that every time I put a contingency in a contract, I'm reducing my chances of getting it accepted. Especially if I'm dealing with banks or government sellers. They just don't look favorably at clouded contracts.

While most potential buyers are making offers containing several weasel clauses, and not getting any of those contracts accepted, I'm buying the houses for less than they are offering because my offers are clean. In most cases, they have no contingencies.

I know that sounds dangerous, but is it really? What's the worst that can happen if you make an offer but can't close for some reason? Do they break your kneecaps or hold your kids for ransom? NO! They keep your earnest money deposit. That's the only thing they can do if you've signed a contract that provides for the return of earnest money as the only remedy for default. If your contract contains that clause and you can't close, that's the end of the story. No lawsuits, no broken knees, and no kids held hostage. You lose your deposit and that's it.

Obviously, the best way to reduce the risk of loss is to reduce your deposit. Put up the least amount possible and minimize your risk.

Of course, there are times when a weasel clause is appropriate and perfectly acceptable to the seller. For example, you could make your contract subject to an estimate for repairs if the house has serious damage, or subject to your inspection of the interior if you were unable to gain entry before you made the offer.

Common sense is the key in this area. Once you are proficient at quick analysis of a house prior to making offers, you will seldom need weasel clauses.

COUNTEROFFERS

When you receive a counteroffer, be thankful. It is always preferable to a simple rejection. Many deals may require several offers and counteroffers. Sometimes, contracts begin to show so many markings and changes they become difficult to read. Don't worry. Changes to a contract actually strengthen it, because they demonstrate to an even greater degree a "meeting of minds."

The same basic rules apply in responding to a counteroffer as apply in making the original offer. If the counteroffer shows a great deal of resistance, you may not be dealing with a motivated seller.

NO STANDARD CONTRACT

A contract may say at the top "Standard Contract." In reality, there is no such thing. In each area of the country, there are contract forms approved and promoted by REALTOR® organizations and boards, but this does not mean you as an investor have to use them.

Many investors have their own attorney prepare a contract for frequent use. The document is tailored to the investor's particular style of investing and it has as much right to be called a "standard contract" as any other form.

USING AN ADDENDUM

Many investors have a "standard" addendum they routinely attach to commonly-used contracts. It typically contains their favorite escape clauses and special clauses that favor the investor, such as limitations on liability, subordination, and many other items.

When an addendum is attached to a contract, that contract often appears to the seller to be a more conventional document. In more complex deals, a contract cannot be expected to be static. Other addendums may be added at any time to change the terms.

An addendum is written with opening language that links it to the main contract. It usually states the date of the contract, the names of both seller and buyer, and the address of the property.

The first paragraph might read, "The parties hereto have agreed to the terms of this addendum to the Sales Contract referenced above. The terms of this addendum shall be deemed to be an integral part of said contract, but where the terms of said contract conflict with the terms of this addendum, the terms of this addendum shall control."

Again, I'm going to suggest in most cases, you not use addendum clauses. The more junk you put in a contract, the more reason your seller will have to turn down your offer. Don't use a weasel clause unless absolutely necessary. If circumstances dictate that you must use one, draw up just one all-inclusive clause that will give you time to do whatever it is you need to do to get the deal closed.

An example of an all-inclusive clause: "Subject to buyer's obtaining an appraisal, at buyer's expense, suitable to buyer, within 15 days of acceptance." That covers anything you want it to, doesn't it? If you don't like the appraisal, you don't have to buy the house. You have 15 days to clear up any details and either proceed or back off.

In my opinion, if you take longer than that to release any contingencies, you should be prepared to lose your deposit if you don't close. It's only fair in most cases. Chalk it up to experience and forget it. Instead of crying over spilled milk, go out and milk another cow.

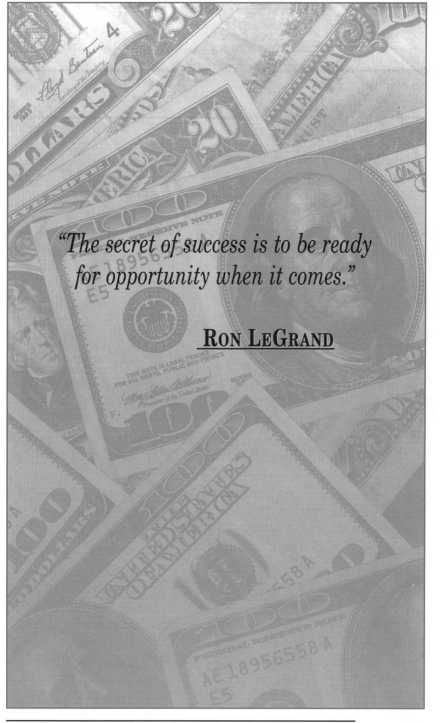

"The secret of success is to be ready for opportunity when it comes."

RON LEGRAND

Section V
Money & Laws

*No man ever achieved worthwhile
success who did not at one time
or other, find himself with at least
one foot hanging well over
the brink of failure*

Napoleon Hill

Where To Get The Money

When I started in real estate in 1982, I thought you had to have money. I had a job, but I was broke. Since then, I have learned you don't need money, credit, or steady employment to do this type of investing. Of course, having a little cash doesn't hurt, but I know some of my readers don't have any, so this chapter is especially for you.

Three basic types of financing are available. **First,** there are bank loans, which are long term, low interest, and tough to qualify for, due to FNMA and FHA guidelines. **Second**, there are alternative sources of short-term money. **Third** is seller financing, which is the ideal source of money as far as an investor is concerned.

SHORTCOMINGS OF BANK LOANS

It seems low-interest, long-term loans are the kind everybody thinks they need and want. The old school of thought was to buy a property cheaply, fix it up, and refinance it. The truth is, if a person had to make a living refinancing every house he bought, he wouldn't be in this business long.

Bank loans have many shortcomings. Sometimes investors, trying to improve their chances of getting loans, will cultivate a particular loan officer, only to discover that the person has quit or the bank has merged with a larger bank that is hostile to investors. Even worse, many banks add "call" provisions to the mortgage note, which means that they can call the loan due at any time for the slightest reason! In today's climate of failing banks, it could be hazardous to your financial health to be dependent on a particular institution.

Another problem is you can not keep going to a bank and borrowing on investment properties. They will cut you off after a few loans. That makes it harder to get a loan of any kind.

Two other key problems are involved. In most cases, the terms of financing are out of your control, and you are personally liable. It is not desirable to be liable for the loan for the full term. As you increase your business and the number of properties you own, being liable for them for the long term is not necessary. Too much debt load can be hazardous, especially since you are still liable for the loan even if someone else assumes it (unless you've gotten a release of liability). Do not expose yourself to this risk by making yourself liable for the loans; do not become involved for the long term if you are liable; stay away, whenever possible, from personally qualifying for loans.

Also, qualifying for a loan can be a challenge. You must prove income and good credit, and subject yourself to a great deal of financial scrutiny. This often poses great difficulties for self-employed investors.

Traditionally, bankers prefer to make investor loans only on occupied, fixed-up properties with long-term leases. With a signed lease, you can get loans for 70% to 80% of the appraised value. But that doesn't help you to buy vacant houses needing repairs. Furthermore, you are fully liable for such loans during the 15, 20, or 30 years it takes to amortize them. Also, these loans are based on the lower of the purchase price or the appraisal within the first year, which in effect penalizes you when you want to negotiate a really low purchase price.

It will take 30 to 60 days to close on this kind of loan. You have to show a positive cash flow or have enough income to offset the debt, and you will usually be forced by the lender to assume a 25% vacancy factor. The property must be in good condition to qualify. The loans are seldom assumable, and even if they are, the person assuming the loan has to go through the same process of qualification as if they were applying for a new loan. These loans will show up on your credit report and impact your borrowing ability in the future.

Finally, most of these loans will not allow the cash-outs investors often want. Most lenders will not allow you to go home with a check. Then there's another problem: I've seen too many investors who think borrowed money is profit and proceed to spend it as if it never has to be repaid. There's no profit until a property is sold.

Considering all these factors, why should you allow yourself to become dependent on banks? Use these loans only for long-term keepers so you can recapture your cash, and only if you can't find another way to get the money you need. You don't even have to do this for your own residence. The only time to go into a bank is to deposit money. Take control of your own financial future!

MORTGAGE BROKERS AND SHORT-TERM MONEY

The best place to get short-term money is through a mortgage broker who knows what will and will not work. Brokers know what they can get in the market today. Some of them have access to private funds that require no qualifying by the borrower. Equity in the house is the only concern. These brokers will be a valuable asset when you use their services.

Remember, when I started, I had no credit. I had no choice but to utilize whatever funds were available, so I found a broker who would loan 50% of the appraised price regardless of my financial condition. He charged me 10% of every loan I made, and I paid 18% interest. The costs were high, but the rewards were worth it. I soon learned that it isn't the cost of money that counts, but the availability of it.

Because I had access to those funds, I bought up junkers and made thousands of dollars in profit on each. Let me ask you a question. Would you rather pay a mortgage broker 10% of your loan or pay a partner 50% of your deal? Tough choice, isn't it?

Of course, if you have the money to buy a house, you don't need to take out a loan or be concerned about loan fees.

Mortgage brokers work on a commission. They do not get paid unless you get paid. If you use private money, get used to the idea of paying high points and consider it a cost of doing business.

You can get a high-interest loan and still make money. Remember, it's not the cost of the money that matters; it's the availability that counts. When I went into business, I borrowed on 76 loans at 18% interest, 50% LTV ratio, six months' interest prepayment penalty, seven-year balloon payment, and 10 points up front to the broker who put up the money. I still made money on every single deal! Most of the houses were in poor condition, so I used the borrowed money to repair them before I sold them. You can do that with those kinds of loans.

You need a mortgage broker whenever you are going to deal in short-term money, unless you are going to develop your own private lenders. If you do you will save 10% brokerage to the broker and you might even get a lower rate. Develop your own list of lenders. If the house needs repairs, you may not get all the money at once. Some of it may be escrowed to allow the repairs to be made. As this is a common technique, it will benefit you to understand what it means and how to calculate it.

Here's an example: Suppose your offer is accepted for $15,000 cash on a property whose value after repairs is $45,000. The as-is value is $35,000, and the estimated repair costs are $4,000. You know you can get a loan from a private investor for 50% LTV of the fixed-up property.

Value after fix-up	**$45,000**
As-is value	**$35,000**
Repair estimate	**$ 4,000**
Maximum loan amount*	**$ 22,500**

The cost of the loan**** $ 3,000

Net from loan $19,500

* ($45,000 x 50%) = $22,500
** **closing costs**

The problem is the loan is based on the after-repaired value. The broker will write the loan for $22,500 even though the property hasn't been repaired yet. You'll close the loan for $22,500. You'll pay the costs on $22,500, and you'll start paying interest on $22,500 as of that day.

The lender, however, will escrow 50% of the difference between the as-is and the after-repaired value. In this case, that amount would be 50% of $10,000, i.e., the $45,000 repaired value minus the $35,000 as-is value. The escrow would then be 50% of $10,000 because it is a 50% LTV loan.

•Held in escrow 50% of difference: $5,000

The closing agent will hold the $5,000 in escrow until the work is completed. If we would normally net $19,500 on this loan, we will now net $14,500 at closing, i.e., $19,500 - $5,000 = $14,500.

After the work is done, the mortgage broker will send an appraiser out to look at the finished house and, if all the work is satisfactorily completed, he will give you the $5,000 that was in escrow.

In the above example, we need $15,000 cash to buy the house and $4,000 to repair it. We need $19,000, but we are going to get only $14,500 from the loan at closing, so we would construct our offer this way:

"Mr. Seller, I'm going to give you $15,000 for this house. I'll give you $10,000 at closing and $5,000 within 60 days. Will that be alright?"

"Yes, that would be OK."

In doing this, we are fully protected. We would get $14,500 from loan proceeds. We would then give the seller $10,000 at closing and still have $4,500 left over. We need $4,000 to repair the house, so we are able to keep the $500 that is left over. Now we have protected ourselves. The seller does not have a problem getting his money. We do not have to get another loan to pay the $5,000 we owe him, because it is sitting in escrow. It will be paid as soon as the house is repaired and we get the money out of escrow.

To make this work, the seller will hold a second mortgage on this property for 60 days because we obtained the first mortgage from a private investor through a mortgage broker. This is known as "subordination." It is a useful tool for any investor.

Another way is simply to give the seller a promissory note for his balance that's not secured against the house. Even better, just have the closing agent prepare an agreement that will allow your seller to pick up the money in escrow after you have completed the work. The seller should feel safe knowing the money can't be released until the work is completed, especially if he or she has the right to collect it directly from the escrow.

You will find the amount to be escrowed varies from lender to lender. Some lenders may require as much as 100% escrow for repairs. Others may require only 50% escrow for repairs. Often, the lender will not escrow 50% of the difference, but instead will escrow what you say it will cost to repair the house. For example, if you can show the repairs will cost $4,000, some lenders will escrow that amount. You don't have much say-so in the matter. Therefore, the golden rule applies: "Those who have the gold make the rules."

Generally, the money these mortgage brokers find for us comes from private individuals. The only consideration for one of these private loans is the LTV ratio. The length of the loan may vary, but generally it's possible to go up to 15 years with a five-year "cap" on the loan. This means that a lot of brokers will amortize the loans as if they were for 15 years, but, in reality, there is a balloon payment due in five years or less. They don't want the risk of having the money out for 15 years. The money is very liquid; they can sell the note easily if they wish, or receive payments for a short period of time

This short-term money is valuable to us as investors. If you get a good deal on a house, you can get a loan on the value of the house, not what you paid for it. A private investor is very different from a bank, because he usually doesn't care what you paid for the property. There is none of the usual verification ordeal. The only verification is the value of the property. You do not need good credit, these loans are not recorded on your credit report, and there is usually no qualifying. Private investors don't care about your personality or personal history. They are only concerned about LTV ratio and the safety of their investment. A good deal of the time they don't even check your income or credit!

As an example, suppose you buy a house worth $50,000 for $30,000 and you obtain a loan for $25,000. The private individual who makes the loan through the mortgage broker would be in good shape if you were to default because he would take back a $50,000 house. It's hard to lose in a 50% LTV situation. This is why private lenders like to make loans to us, those loans are very safe. Once you understand what you can borrow through mortgage brokers or your own lenders, you will know how to construct better offers.

In the following example, you'll see how to provide all the money needed for a purchase so that it is totally "no money down."

I once found a house with a sale price of $15,000, all cash. The property was in excellent shape and didn't need any work. It would appraise for $32,000 to $35,000. The house was put under contract for $14,500, all cash. A mortgage broker, who was also a private investor, was shown the property and was told that I wanted to borrow $16,000, secured by the property. (It was necessary to borrow $16,000 to cover the closing cost so the house could be bought with no money down.)

The mortgage broker inquired about the sale price. Upon hearing it was $15,000, he said he would loan only $15,000 on this house. I knew that the broker was getting a brokerage fee, and there were going to be other closing costs. I was going to net

$13,500. Knowing I was paying $14,500 and was going to net $13,500, I had to come up with $1,000 out of pocket. I called the seller and told him I could get only a $13,500 loan on the house. So I asked the seller to lower the price $1,000 or take a $1,000 note for $50 a month at 0% interest until the $1,000 was paid.

The seller checked with his partner and agreed to take the $1,000 note. I left that closing with a check for $147.00 with no money invested. I sold the house to an investor for $3,000 cash to mortgage a few days later.

Be careful if you have had problems in the past that lead to a judgment against you. You shouldn't take title to property if you do. As soon as you buy any property and take title to it, the judgment may attach to the property. The only thing you can do is take title in some other name, usually a trust or corporation. This way you can get a loan and not put the property at risk of having a judgment attached.

Here are a few more details about getting money through your mortgage broker. An appraisal usually will be necessary even if the loan is 50% to 55% LTV. If it is less than 50% LTV, say about 20% LTV, an appraisal may not be necessary. It takes five days to two weeks to close the loan, a relatively short time in which to obtain money.

With private loans, the property can be vacant or in poor condition. However, if the property is in poor condition, don't expect to get a loan based on its worth after repairs and be able to take home all that money at closing without escrow of repair funds. That will not happen.

Expect to pay 15% to 18% interest for money obtained through a mortgage broker. Base your business on these rates. It may seem high, but it is a small price to pay to have access to the money, especially if there is no other way to obtain funds. Eighteen percent interest will seem insignificant after a few deals. If you want access to the money necessary to put these deals together, you have to pay the price.

Sometimes you will have personal liability for these loans, and sometimes you won't. Some lenders will require a personal signature for corporate loans and some won't. The reason for this money is to get in, get out, and pay it off. Personal liability for a loan of this type is not nearly as important as personal liability on an 80% LTV loan. On these low LTV loans, personal liability just doesn't make that much difference, because it is already so safe for the lender. Nobody will be coming after you for a deficiency judgment, even if they were to foreclose on a loan, because the loan is only 50% of the value of the property. There is just too much equity in the property to have a deficiency. And the lender knows that these loans, for the most part, will be out for only a few weeks to a few months.

SELLER FINANCING

Seller financing is absolutely the best financing of all. Your income potential will increase dramatically if you use it properly. Seller financing is being used anytime the seller of a property takes back part of the purchase price in the form of a mortgage. The seller simply collects payments on the mortgage. It's no more complicated than that.

Why do you need it?

- **First,** it's cheaper. You can't get a 0% to 6% interest rate any other way. If you know how to ask for it, you can routinely get 0% or a greatly reduced interest rate.

- **Second**, you do not pay any points or origination fees with seller financing.

- **Third**, you can easily use special clauses in your mortgage note that are profitable to investors. For example, you can be sure that you will be able to transfer the mortgage with a substitution of collateral clause. You can also have the right to subordinate the seller financing to new financing. Both of these techniques are discussed on the following page.

- **Fourth**, an excellent reason for seller financing is there are no due-on-sale or balloon-payment provisions in the mortgage if you do not put them there.

By contrast, all conventional loans have a due-on-sale clause, plus charges for points, application fees, and appraisal charges, and many have prepayment penalties. This puts the lender in control of the loan. When we do seller financing, we don't put the lender in control. We stay in control. The provisions you insert into a privately-held mortgage are entirely between you and the seller. For instance, if we buy a property and the seller carries a second mortgage, you may not put a late penalty in it. Be careful with contracts used by REALTORS® there is usually a space to indicate due-on-sale or not due-on-sale. The problem lies in the fact that they also call for you to qualify to the seller. I white this out on the contracts I use.

Be careful about the wording of the contract because it will govern the way the closing agent handles the transaction. This can work for you or against you. If there is no due-on-sale or a late penalty in the contract, then it shouldn't be on your note.

As an example, let me tell you about a property for which I paid too much and still received a good deal. I paid $35,000 for it, putting $5,000 down and giving the seller a $30,000 mortgage subordinated to a new first mortgage. The interest rate on the mortgage was 0%, and I am paying him $250 a month until it's paid. That's the way it was negotiated going in. (I even negotiated for the contents of the house, and later had a garage sale.)

The house is in a low-income part of town, and the seller believed it to be worth $35,000. Actually, it was worth $45,000 repaired, and needed $3,000 to $4,000 in repairs. The owner had been trying to sell the house for a year, but had received no offers. He owned it free and clear, was moving, and just wanted to get rid of it.

I believe I paid him too much money, but it didn't matter a great deal in this instance. I paid him $5,000 down and borrowed $18,000 on a new first mortgage. This left me owing him $30,000 on a second mortgage for a total of $48,000. On the other hand, I am paying him $250 a month, and every bit of that is principal. The second mortgage is being paid off at about $3,000 a year. I've owned it for four years and have already paid down the note by $12,000.

MORE ON ZERO INTEREST LOANS

Even though I paid retail for the above-mentioned house, I will still make money because of the seller's financing at 0% interest. That is what makes this deal a good deal. When seller financing is done correctly, you can solve negative cash flow. It wouldn't work with a $30,000 loan from an institution such as a bank or mortgage company.

I don't talk about interest unless the seller brings it up. I tell the seller that I will pay him $100 a month for 150 months starting in three months. It is very rare for a seller to ask about interest when the terms are presented this way. The interest rate is not the seller's prime concern unless you make it his prime concern. If the seller had wanted 9% interest, I would have tried for a promise to keep the payments at $250 a month by negotiating a lower interest for a longer time. If the seller was really hard nosed about it, I just wouldn't buy the house. The seller doesn't really have much choice since he would have trouble selling the house as it is anyway, and I really don't have to buy it because there are too many other deals out there.

If you don't talk about interest, the seller may not talk about it either because it's the last thing on his or her mind. Sellers are interested in how much they are going to receive at closing, when they can close, and what their purchase price is going to be. Never mention interest rates and you will be surprised how often the seller won't either, provided you are dealing with a motivated seller.

WRAPAROUND MORTGAGES

I couldn't talk about seller financing without mentioning wraparound mortgages. They may become an important tool for you in selling houses and sometimes even in buying them.

Simply stated, a wrap is a seller carryback loan that surrounds or "wraps" already-existing financing. You will be collecting an incoming payment from your buyer and paying out an outgoing payment, or payments, to your lender. It is to be hoped for that your incoming payment will be larger than your outgoing payment. If it's not, you need to attend another seminar on seller financing.

For example, let's say you sell a house for $60,000 with owner financing. You get a $5,000 down payment and carry back a $55,000 mortgage paying $550 per month. You owe a $30,000 first mortgage to an institution for which you are paying $300 per month, and a $10,000 second mortgage to a private seller to whom you are paying $75 per month. So in this example, you are collecting $550 per month and paying out $375 per month for a monthly net of $175. In addition, you owe $40,000, and you are owed $55,000, so you have an equity position of $15,000. The $55,000 wraps around the $40,000 so the total debt on the property is only $55,000, not $95,000. The $40,000 is part of the $55,000, not in addition to it.

In addition to the monthly spread and the immediate equity position, you also should be receiving a monthly equity buildup because, normally, the $55,000 the buyer owes you should be being paid down much more slowly than the $40,000 you owe. Sooner or later your outgoing payments will be paid off while your incoming payments keep on coming. This is assuming that you don't get paid off in cash, which is usually what happens. What a problem that would be!

LAND CONTRACTS, CONTRACT FOR DEED, AGREEMENT FOR DEED

These terms are used everywhere and mean essentially the same thing. Briefly, they mean a promise to pay. Until the debt is paid, the seller retains title and the buyer receives an equitable interest in the property. The buyer feels like an owner and acts like an owner, but legally does not become a title holder until the terms of the contract are satisfied, at which time the seller actually deeds the property to the buyer.

This method of sale is widely used in some states because it makes the repossession process much simpler than foreclosing. In some areas, a buyer can be removed from the house within 30 days for non-payment, with no more legal process required than an eviction.

These contracts can also be good tools to avoid due-on-sale clauses that permit a lender to call the loan due on transfer. In some states, the property isn't considered transferred until a deed is delivered.

Closing costs are another factor. Since a land contract isn't much more than a glorified lease option, there are minimal closing costs. Usually, there is only the cost of checking the title, plus attorney fees. For this reason, some investors choose to buy on a land contract just long enough to sell the house, thus avoiding dual costs. The seller then delivers a deed directly to the new buyer. In some areas, this procedure provides big savings.

SPLIT FUNDING

The Split Funding method is well suited to very short-term Quick-Turn deals. As seller financing goes, it is a simple technique. The investor offers a small amount of the cash to close the deal, with the remaining amount due months later. No interest is paid and only one lump sum payment is due. You can buy a lot of houses with this one technique. The investor repairs the house and sells it retail, which means the buyer obtains a new loan, either FHA, VA, or conventional. The investor then pays off the seller financing that he negotiated earlier. He just convinces the seller to take a little money now with the rest paid in full in six months, or whatever they negotiate.
Here's an example:

	$50,000 asking price
	$ 5,000 repairs
	$75,000 property value after repairs
The deal:	$45,000 purchase price
	$ 5,000 down payment
	$40,000 no interest, no payments, all due in six months

Most people will not use this method to buy a house because they think they need a lot of cash. But the deal really only took $5,000, and hundreds in interest were saved.

If you can't sell the property in six months, just renegotiate the payment. However, you don't need to wait six months since the note can be renegotiated at any time in the future, even if it's five days after the closing. The only agreement is between the buyer and the seller. Whenever you have two private people involved, there is always room to negotiate.

Another possibility is to give the seller $2,000 toward the principal and get an extension on the $40,000 payment for another three to six months, or whatever you agree on.

Seller financing made this deal possible, but working through a REALTOR® wouldn't be a problem. You might have to put a little more down so the REALTOR® can receive a commission and the seller also gets a little cash. With this method, you can use the REALTOR'S® MLS book to look for deals and make offers. Look for properties that are in need of repair. I used a REALTOR® to make this kind of offer on the first 22 houses that I bought.

The key advantage to this approach is it permits you to make more of those all-cash offers sellers always want. Even if they don't get it all at closing, it's paid shortly thereafter. Here's an example. I was called about a house with an asking price of $30,000.

After repairs of approximately $3,000, it appeared the value would be about $48,000. I handled this one with split funding. I gave some cash at closing and some cash later to satisfy the seller's needs. That gave me time to sell the house.

My offer: $20,000 purchase price
$ 2,000 cash down payment
$18,000 balance due in six months
with no interest and no payments

Also note that I could have made a second offer, at the same time, of $15,000 all cash at closing, because I knew I could net at least that amount if I had to borrow it from a private lender.

The offers were stated this way:

"Mr. Seller, I'll give you $20,000 with $2,000 down, and $18,000 within six months, or I'll give you $15,000 cash at the closing table. Which do you prefer?"

In this case, he took the higher, split-funded offer. It is usually better to make both offers at the same time and let the seller decide which one works best for them. In our two offers, either one will work for us. Even though the seller is asking $30,000, we offer him $15,000, all cash, and see if he will take the offer. Cash talks! Neither of these offers is complicated. They don't have a subordination clause or any other difficult-to-understand terms.

I was once called about a property that was owned free and clear. The purchase price was $20,000. I gave $4,000 down, with $16,000 due in 120 days, no interest, no payments, just the principal balance payment.

The property appraised for $42,000, after $3,000 worth of work. I didn't want to do the work, so I sold the property for $27,000. The buyer put $6,000 down. I was able to sell the house before I had even bought it. The buyer and seller were at the closing on the same day, but thankfully, not in the same room!

I took $4,000 from the $6,000 I received from the new buyer and gave that to the original seller. A total of $2,000 went into my pocket at closing. The new buyer paid $27,000, and after the $6,000 at closing, still owed $21,000 to me. After I gave the original seller $4,000 down, I still owed $16,000. When the new buyer paid his debt of $21,000 to me, I paid the $16,000 to the seller and made another $5,000 net on the property.

This deal worked because I gave the seller some cash at closing and the rest in 120 days, with no interest and no payments. Split funding the payment, by giving some down and the rest later, is one of the secrets to short-term Quick-Turns. I had a contract. I told the seller exactly what I was going to do, and I did it. People usually have no problem waiting six to 12 months for their money if you ask them.

SUBORDINATION

"Subordination" is a tool that can make a lot of money for you. The right of subordination is a clause you can insert into your contract. It permits you to get a new first mortgage, even though you already have seller financing in place. In other words, subordination occurs when the seller agrees to take back a second mortgage and allows you to get a new first mortgage on the property.

It works best with houses carrying low or no mortgages. When properly used, subordination combined with seller financing makes short-term Quick-Turn deals possible with the least amount of cash, or even no cash. Many times it even allows you to bring home thousands of dollars the day you buy a house. Subordination also serves as a useful financing tool to make properties saleable to people who might not otherwise qualify.

Before I explain this, let's examine the clause you should incorporate into your purchase and sale agreement to make subordination possible. This clause is included in the contract, or in the addendum to the contract:

> **Subordination Clause**: Seller understands that the buyer(s) or assigns will be getting a first mortgage of a maximum of the appraised value less the purchase money mortgage to the seller(s). Seller(s) hereby acknowledge that they understand that the purchase money second mortgage they will hold is junior to the above-mentioned first.

If an owner sells you his house for $30,000, with $14,000 down, and he agrees to take a subordinated second mortgage back at $16,000 you have the right to go get a new first mortgage on the property without paying the owner his $16,000 at that time. Instead, his mortgage will remain a second, and you will get a new first. You will pay him whatever payments you agreed to pay him, but he does not have to get paid off at the time that you get the new loan.

If you read the clause carefully, you'll see that it protects the seller by preventing you from over-financing the property. The total of your new first and his seller carry-back second can't exceed the value of the house.

Let's examine a typical example of the use of the subordination clause. I once talked with a seller who was asking $30,000 for his house. The owner indicated he would hold paper, that is, he would be willing to take payments for his equity. I knew that his house was really worth $40,000 after repairs, and needed $3,000 in repairs. I made an offer of $25,000 as the purchase price, of which $5,000 would be in cash and the remaining $20,000 would be on a subordinated mortgage.

This meant that the owner was willing to take a $20,000 mortgage that he agreed would be in a second position, giving me the right to go out and put a new first mortgage on the property. The seller was willing to do this to get the $5,000 cash and get rid of his house.

Next, I applied for and obtained a new first mortgage for $15,000, using private lenders, and let the seller hold the second mortgage for $20,000. The property was then financed for a total of $35,000. As it was worth $40,000, it was not over-financed. Of the $15,000 first mortgage I received, I subtracted the $5,000 cash down payment, the $3,000 for repairs, and another $2,000 in closing costs, retaining $5,000 net cash.

$20,000	seller financing is subordinated and becomes a second mortgage
$15,000	new first mortgage, borrowed on $40,000 value
- $ 5,000	down payment
- $ 3,000	repairs
- $ 2,000	closing costs
$ 5,000	net cash

Because the house was worth $40,000, it was easy to get the $15,000 new first mortgage. I sold the house on a wraparound mortgage and made sure the first and second got paid.

I didn't tell the seller how much I was going to borrow on the first, and he didn't ask. I made it clear to him, however, that I was going to put a new first mortgage on the house. The title company also made it clear to him, so he couldn't come back later and cry foul. The seller must be highly motivated and the property in need of repairs for you to be able to do this. And the property must have a lot of equity. This deal can work even if there is an existing first on the property, and the seller agrees to take a third, allowing you to go out and get a new second, as long as the payments allow adequate positive cash flow.

The seller must understand the subordination! When I do a subordination deal, I tell the seller exactly what I am going to do, why I am going to do it, and, sometimes, how much I am going to borrow. If he doesn't like it, he can go find someone else to buy his house. You can't do this without the seller's knowing what is going on. The title company or attorney will not close the deal unless they know the seller understands.

Why do sellers take a subordination? It works for them for three reasons: **First**, they are extremely motivated. **Second**, they usually have a junker of a house they can't sell, or they don't have the funds for repair. **Third**, in most cases, they are getting more money from you than they would get if they sold all cash to some other buyer. Even though you aren't paying them all cash, quite often the sales price means more to the seller than the amount of immediate money.

In 9 of 10 subordinations I have done, I have made an alternative, all-cash offer at the same time, and I always documented it in writing. If there is ever a dispute later where a buyer claims he was taken advantage of, you can say, "I gave this man a choice of three different ways I would buy his house. He picked this way." More often than not, sellers will take the subordination deal rather than the low, all-cash offer. A motivated seller has a reason to take a subordination deal. If you fail to ask, however, you won't get anyone to do it.

Let me tell you about another deal I negotiated in a low-income part of town. The seller thought his house was worth $30,000. In fact, it was probably worth $45,000 repaired, and needed $3,000 to $4,000 in repairs.

He had been trying to sell this house for a year. He had called all the house buyers who advertised in the newspaper.

None of them made him an offer. He had had it with this house. He was tired of talking to people about it. He was tired of taking phone calls about it. He was tired of paying for ads and getting no response. He was sick and tired of looking at this piece of junk that smelled disgusting and needed a ton of work.

He just wanted someone to come and solve his problem. He believed his house to be worth $30,000, but he was more than willing to take $20,000. I discovered that he had inherited the property from his aunt three years before; he owned it free and clear. When I went to see him, I was the only one who had ever talked seriously to him about buying this property.

This is how the conversation went:

"Mr. Seller, I can buy your property two ways. I can give you $10,000, all cash. That's way number one."

I wrote this out on paper for him. I did not put it in contract form. I wrote it on a legal pad with a big "$10,000 Cash." Before telling him the second option, I wrote the number "2" on the page.

"For option two, Mr. Seller, I can give you $20,000, with $5,000 down, and $15,000 on a second mortgage, paying you $100 a month with the first payment due in four months. Understand now, Mr. Seller, since this house is in such bad shape, I have to have the right to go get a new first mortgage on it to raise the capital to put it back into condition. My experience tells me after I do that, Mr. Seller, I am probably going to put a mortgage on this property somewhere in the neighborhood of $20,000. OK? You understand I have to make a profit at what I do. Or I am not willing to do this. This is a big job, isn't it?"
"Yes, OK."

"What I am going to do is buy your house, repair it, then get a mortgage on it for $20,000 to $25,000, depending on what it's worth when I'm done."
"Yes."

"OK. You see, that is the only way I can buy your house, Mr. Seller. I'll start your payments four months from the time we close. But you need to understand what I am doing and why I am doing it. OK? If that's a problem for you, Mr. Seller, I would rather not do it. Maybe you would be better off taking the $10,000 cash offer. What do you think?"

"No, I'll take choice number two."

"OK, sign here, Mr. Seller."

It was the seller who told me which offer he wanted. I didn't try to make the decision for him. From the above conversation, we can understand why the seller would be willing to take offer number two.

Here is another example of an interesting deal involving subordination. The purchase price was $18,000, with $2,000 down; the seller agreed to carry a subordinated second mortgage of $16,000 at $125 a month with 0% interest until paid. When I sold the property, the new buyer obtained a $15,000 first on it and took over the $16,000 second. There was then a total of $31,000 owed on the property, and it was worth $32,000 to $33,000. I gave the new buyer $3,000 at closing to repair the house, then made him sign that the repairs would be done and he would take personal responsibility and liability on the $16,000 second. With a $15,000 loan, a $3,000 rebate, and a cost of $2,000 to close, the profit was $8,000 net. My knowledge of financing made this transaction work.

The seller agreed to this deal because the house was in a weak selling area. It was in poor condition, and the seller didn't have any other offers. Nobody else offered an alternative solution to the problem. I was paid well for problem solving.

Incidentally, investors are not the only ones who profit from subordination. Builders also use the subordination technique. They make the landowner's mortgage note subordinate to the construction loan, and when the permanent financing is put in place, the landowner gets paid off. I didn't invent the technique, but I use it because it is such an incredible, cash-generating tool.

SUBSTITUTION OF COLLATERAL

Substitution of collateral simply means I am taking an existing mortgage on one property and transferring it to another. I am substituting the collateral from one property to another.

As usual, we have to find a motivated seller or we can't make the deal. We should look for a seller who has a reason to do a substitution of collateral. Without a motivated seller, none of this will work. Here is an example of some typical numbers:

- $30,000 asking price on house "A"
- $3,000 repairs
- $40,000 value after fix-up

My **offer** was:

- $25,000 purchase price for house "A"
- $5,000 down payment
- $20,000 first to seller with substitution
  of collateral

We have a lot of equity in house "A." We intend to profit on that equity by repairing the house and finding a cash buyer for $40,000. We have to have another property, however, to be able to substitute the collateral. We will call that house "B." House "B" is a house that we own, which has enough equity to support the $20,000 we're transferring from house "A." It has a first mortgage of $25,000 and is worth $45,000. We ask the seller to take $5,000 cash and move the remainder of the first that he holds, $15,000 in this case, from house "A" to house "B," at which time it will become a second. We can do this at the time we close the sale on house "A," or any time prior.

The **negotiation** goes as follows:

> **"Mr. Seller, I owe you $20,000 on house 'A.' What I'd like to do, instead of taking 20 years to pay you as we agreed on in the beginning, is to give you $5,000 now, in cash. Could you use $5,000 cash now, Mr. Seller?"**
> *"Yes."*

> **"OK, instead of leaving the mortgage on house 'A,' what we're going to do, with your permission, is to take the remaining $15,000 I will then owe you on house "A," and take our payment that I was paying you, $200 a month, and reduce it down to $150 a month. Then we'll move it to my house over on "B" street. My house over on "B" street is worth about $45,000. I have a $25,000 first on it. So I'm asking you to take a $15,000 second on house "B," but I'm giving you $5,000 to make it worth your while. Is that fair?**
> *"Yes, that seems fair to me."*

I'm still going to make payments to the seller, but in a lesser amount. I gave the seller $5,000 cash to convince him to do this. I may or may not agree to this prior to purchasing the seller's house. If I had agreed to it, there would have been a substitution of collateral document attached to the mortgage I gave to the seller, and there would be a clause in the contract that says I have the right to substitute this collateral at a later date. You will find a sample of this document in Appendix F.

I am not really asking the seller, in this example, to do anything he had not already agreed on as a condition of the original purchase of this property.

What if I didn't agree on this condition, or didn't want to bring it up at the beginning of negotiations to buy the property from the seller? I can still do it, because $5,000 carries a lot of negotiation punch. I possibly could have done it with $1,000, $2,000, or $3,000. In this example, I am paying the seller 25% of what I owe him. Why wouldn't the seller do it? He most likely would because of the up-front cash. I offered him $5,000 to move his mortgage instead of discounting it because I could put more cash in my pocket by moving the mortgage.

Maybe I could have gotten the seller to discount the mortgage by $5,000 and paid him off the $15,000, but I would only be putting $5,000 more in my pocket. However, if I pay the seller $5,000 and move the $15,000, I would be putting $15,000 more in my pocket. The above deal would work this way, since house 'A' is free and clear after I move the seller's mortgage to house 'B.'

$40,000 cash sale from someone who buys it FHA or VA
-$ 5,000 original down payment
-$ 5,000 additional payment to seller for moving mortgage
-$ 1,500 closing costs
-$ 3,000 repairs
$25,500 cash in my pocket

Not bad for a house that sold for only $40,000!

I found a buyer who obtained a $40,000 FHA loan. I got back my $5,000 original down payment and collected the seller's $5,000 prepayment for the right to substitute at the closing table. Since the money wasn't disbursed until the sale closed, I didn't have to come up with the money to get the seller to do this.

At closing, I received the money from the buyer, who had obtained an FHA loan. The buyer brought a check for $40,000 to the closing. I already had an agreement to move this mortgage, signed by the seller, saying I owed him $5,000. I handed this agreement to the closing agent. The closing agent wrote a check to the seller for $5,000 and had the seller come down, after closing, to sign a substitution of collateral form.

The mortgage was no longer on his house. It had been transferred to house "B," about which I gave the title company a legal description. The seller got his check, and I got my substitution of collateral form signed. The title company could then issue a clean title to house "A," because the seller's mortgage was no longer on the property.

I wouldn't let the seller know I was selling house "A" — and I wouldn't ever approach the seller to substitute the collateral — until I had a buyer for house "A" and was ready to close.

Another twist on this deal was that house "B," which was worth $45,000, had a $25,000 first mortgage and now the seller's $15,000 second mortgage. That makes house "B" financed to 90% with no points and no qualifying. It would be a good house to sell for $45,000 with $5,000 down and a wraparound mortgage created for $40,000. Three years later, if the buyer wants to sell and pay off the mortgage, I can go to the seller and substitute the mortgage again, or pay it off at a discount. With private sellers, as long as you owe, you have flexibility.

You can't do a substitution of collateral without seller financing. It is not complicated to put into effect, but the seller must be informed and aware of what you are doing. You can't sneak this by the seller. Also, make certain that the property to which you move the mortgage is not over financed.

Here is another example of how this technique can put cash in your pocket. I purchased a house for $19,000. I gave the seller an $8,000 down payment, let the seller take back a mortgage note for $11,000, then signed a substitution of collateral form with him.

When I moved the mortgage, I didn't give the seller anything to encourage him to move it. I did about $5,000 worth of repairs to the property and sold it for $41,000. I obtained a new loan for the buyer equal to $32,000, and I took back a $4,900 second mortgage, with the buyer's putting down $4,100.

At the time I did this, I had the seller move the $11,000 mortgage to another property. I put $11,000 more cash in my pocket than if I had paid off the first mortgage held by the original seller. These things work, but only if you ask. The original seller had agreed to the substitution of collateral because her house was in poor condition and was located in a bad part of town, and I gave her the price she was asking.

Both the subordination agreement and the substitution of collateral agreement forms will be filled out by the closing agent. You don't have to know how to complete them.

RAISING MONEY FAST WITHOUT BORROWING

When you have the cash, it is so much easier to invest! Those who enjoy instant access to large sums of cash do not need to work with lenders for purchase money. Most of us, however, need to raise the cash to do the deal. We have already discussed ways to reduce the need for cash by split funding, and how to make it easier to raise cash through a seller by using subordination and substitution of collateral. Now, let's talk about raising cash fast, without going to a lender or a seller for a real estate loan.

The most obvious way to accomplish this is just to ask a partner — often another investor — to put up the cash. Before you approach a partner, however, it's wise to have all your numbers worked out and the entire deal planned very carefully, using conservative estimates. It is customary to split equally with the partner whatever profit is made.

Earlier in this book, I told you about investment groups. That's where you can find a great many potential partners. You also can advertise in the newspaper. Many people in every city in America have money to invest in real estate, but they do not have the time or knowledge.

Whenever you want to make an all-cash offer, and don't think you want to use any of the methods listed above, whether it be loans, split funding, subordination, or whatever, you can always team up with a person who has the cash. If you can find the deals, there is an abundance of people to work with you as partners. All that's really necessary are knowledge and persistence.

One clever way to raise a down payment is to trade something you already own. Anything of value, such as a motor home, car, truck, land, or appliances, can be traded for a down payment on property. You can even trade knowledge or services. Find out what the seller wants. See if you can take care of those wants without cash.

Another way to raise cash fast, one that is far too often overlooked, is the careful use of credit cards. Credit cards are an excellent source of money. People worry about the high interest rate, but when you're in a short-term, Quick-Turn deal, the actual difference in interest dollars is very little.

As I mentioned previously, when I started in this business, I made 76 loans at 18% interest. The availability of the money was important, not its cost. I recommend, however, that you not use credit cards to buy property unless you pay the cards back with the profits. Otherwise, you could get into big financial trouble. But if you use cards wisely, they are an excellent line of credit.

Get as high a credit line as possible on your cards. If you have a $5,000 line of credit, write to ask for a $10,000 limit. Get more credit cards before you actually need them. Don't apply for more than three in any one month. That would necessitate too many credit checks at one time and cause turndowns. Just get a couple at a time. There are thousands of sources of credit cards in this country, many of which have no annual fee. And some of them don't even check your credit.

If you acquire ten cards and each has a credit limit of just $2,000, that's the equivalent of a $20,000 line of credit. If you gradually raise the limits on those cards to $5,000 each, through careful use and periodic asking for increases, you then have access to $50,000 in instant cash.

As your income grows, many of these credit cards can be raised to as high as $25,000 each. Almost all credit cards now permit cash advances up to the credit limit. Since there is no limit on how many credit cards you can have, low initial credit limits need not stop you, and access to $100,000 or more in "Fast Cash" is possible. How many all-cash deals could you do with access to that much cash?

Even if you have poor credit history, you can acquire a secured credit card simply by making a deposit equal to your credit limit. In time, this limit will be increased with no additional deposit.

MAKING THE SELLER YOUR PARTNER

This section could just as well have been titled "How to buy a big, expensive home that you thought you couldn't afford." The main difficulty in owning an expensive home is that you cannot buy it with no money down and maintain a reasonable monthly payment. The lower your down payment, the higher the monthly payment will be, and that could cause payment problems. Equity participation is a technique whereby you can make the seller your partner and reduce your monthly payment to a comfortable amount.

Suppose, for example, you wanted to live in a $300,000 house in an area where the average price was $100,000, but you could only afford payments of $1,000 per month. As a general rule of thumb, one would expect payments on a house of that value to be about $3,000. The strategy is as follows: **First**, find a large home with a lot of equity in it. Look for a flexible owner who does not need his cash out of the house, and who is willing to take monthly payments for his equity.

Many houses are free and clear or have a large equity. If the property is free and clear, the chances are good that an owner doesn't need cash from his house. Look for a house that would be hard to move. The payments, alone, on a $300,000 house would put a lot of people out of the market. Look for a house that needs some repairs.

The **second** step is to negotiate a purchase price somewhat below the retail value. Suppose you negotiate a price of $250,000. The conversation might go like this:

"Mr. Seller, I have a way to buy your house and pay you more in the long run, if you are willing to take less per month now. Are you interested in hearing more about this?

"Yes! Tell me more."

"Well, I want to make your house my residence, so I can buy it now for $250,000 and give you back a mortgage, if we can agree on the terms. My only problem is I just can't handle the normal monthly payment that comes with a house in this price range. So what I am proposing we do is, I'll pay you $10,000 down and you take back a mortgage for $240,000. But instead of a high payment that I can't afford, I'll give you $1000 per month

which you call interest. I'll make you this interest-only payment each month and still owe you all the principal.

"Now, I know this is a low payment, so in return, I'm willing to compensate you this way:

"I'll do the repairs at my expense and maintain the house. I'll pay the taxes, insurance, and all other costs on this house until I sell it within a five-year period.

"When I do, I will give you one-half the profit above your $250,000 sales price. I feel that, by that time, the house could sell for $350,000. Therefore, you would not only receive your $240,000 balance, but an additional $50,000 profit in lieu of a higher monthly payment now. I believe this would solve my problem and yours, don't you agree?"

You might have to ask three or four people before you get an acceptance. Even if you find people don't trust you enough to do other creative financing, you can still usually lease their house. We don't need to own the house to make money on it. Control is more important than ownership. The owner will get the tax write-off on it. All you have to do is convince the owner you will do what you say you'll do. In effect, you are making the seller your partner.

Place an ad in the paper indicating you're looking for someone with whom to "equity share" a big house. Use the MLS book. Make offers on houses that no one else is looking at — those with high price tags. It is possible to make all kinds of arrangements with a seller. Here is a way to make the seller your partner on a house you don't intend to live in.

"Mr. Seller, I'm not going to buy your house because, frankly, it's too cash intensive, and I don't have the money right now. But this is what I will do. If you'll put up the $3,000 that it takes to repair your house, I'll do all the work, sell it for you, and we'll split the profits above our agreed-on purchase price. Is that fair? I may even make your payments for you while we're doing all this, just to show you my serious intent."

BACK TO BASICS

Of course, let's not forget the absolutely easiest way to raise money with single-family houses. **WHOLESALING**! It just doesn't get any easier than finding the deal and passing it on to someone else who wants a bargain. It's nothing more than a paper shuffle. Easy in, easy out, no loans, no repairs, no partners, no credit, no long holding period, little or no money needed, no risk, and fast cash profits.

Because wholesaling is such an important part of a serious investor's business, we devote a large portion of each Boot Camp to making sure every single student leaves with a thorough understanding of wholesaling. It's what many of them use to create income that triples the amount they earned in their old jobs.

Another example of unforeseen good things happening from unplanned events is the story of Dave Rogers from Anchorage, Alaska. Dave had purchased my course. The story of how that happened is exactly what I meant when I said many opportunities jump in front of us when we least expect them.

Dave had heard about me from a third party, and he got in touch with me. When I mailed Dave my course in May 1992, I also sent him a letter about my upcoming Boot Camp in Houston. What I didn't know then was there was no way Dave could possibly afford to attend. He had serious problems. He had been divorced for a couple of months and was in deep financial trouble. Since I didn't know Dave at the time, there was no way for me to realize he is one of the most stubborn men on earth, and he hates it when he can't do what he wants when he wants.

Apparently, he really wanted to attend the Houston camp, because he borrowed enough money from his ex-wife and ex-mother-in-law to do it. Then, he returned to Alaska, filed for bankruptcy, and drove here to Jacksonville with the few possessions he could load in his crummy car.

In his first three months in a strange town, he used what I had taught him. He purchased $283,000 worth of houses for $92,000, without spending a dime of his own money. Of course, he didn't have any to spend, but the point is, it CAN be done by making the effort to match knowledge with opportunity and taking action. Every one of Dave's deals was wholesaled immediately to produce the instant cash needed.

STRUCTURING AN OFFER

You can use the following two scenarios to practice for making offers before you go out into the real world. Master these scenarios at home first. You must know how to manage the situation when you start for real. It's better if you make a mistake here than in real life. Following the scenarios are some possible answers.

WHAT WOULD YOU OFFER?

SCENARIO 1 : You call about this house after reading an ad in the newspaper. The owners say they inherited the property. It's free and clear, and they are asking $40,000, all cash. After inspection, you determine the house would be worth $50,000 if you spent about $3,000 on it. You have $4,000 left on your Master Card. Your credit is good and you have steady income.

OFFER 1

OFFER 2

OFFER 3

SCENARIO 2 : A REALTOR® brings you a printout about a house whose owners are highly motivated. The house has been neglected. The sellers can't stand each other and are getting a divorce. The listed price is $49,900, and there is a $12,000 mortgage. You inspect the house and conclude it's worth $49,900, but only after you spend about $5,000 to repair it. You are a full-time investor with poor credit, no rich relatives, no rich friends, no credit cards and no provable income, but you know there is a way, because I said so.

OFFER 1

OFFER 2

SCENARIO 1: Answers

Offer 1: ($25,000) all cash. Pay all cash, but get a very low price. Borrow the $25,000 from a finance company and use a charge card to fund the repairs, with the intention of retailing for a large profit. Or, alternatively, simply wholesale the contract to another investor who is better equipped to develop the deal and pick up a quick $3,000 to $5,000 the day he closes. Or, partner with this same investor and pick up an immediate $3,000 finder's fee, then split the retail profit when the house is sold. You do the work; he puts up the money.

Offer 2: ($28,000) $3,000 down, balance due within six months, no payments until due. Use your charge card to buy since it takes only $3,000 down and allows time to implement one of the above solutions. Or take title and sell the property to an owner/occupant as a handyman special for a discounted price of $40,000, leaving you a quick profit of $12,000 without doing any repairs.

Offer 3: ($35,000) $7,000 down, seller to carry back a second mortgage of $28,000 subordinate to a new first mortgage. The second will bear payments of $250 per month at no interest until paid. The house is worth $50,000 after repairs, so you can borrow up to $22,000 on a new first without over-financing ($50,000-$28,000 seller carryback second = $22,000). A $22,000 new first mortgage, less the $7,000 down to seller, less the $3,000 in repairs, leaves $12,000 cash that you can call profit as soon as the house is sold. Now would also be a good time to sell for $54,000 via owner financing with a wraparound mortgage or land contract of $50,000, getting a $4,000 down payment from your buyer.

This means you now have $12,000 left from your loan, plus $4,000 from the buyer for a total of $16,000 profit. Or, alternatively, instead of your getting the new first mortgage, take your buyer to a lender and let him sign on the new loan for $22,000. He will need very little qualifying to get approval for a loan at such a low LTV ratio.

If this is done, you can have your buyer originate a wraparound mortgage to you, for the same $28,000 you owe the seller, except bearing interest. The buyer pays you; you pay the seller, allowing you to keep the interest and protect the seller at the same time.

You will also be setting yourself up for another payday in the future because, sooner or later, the house will get cashed out, giving you the opportunity to either discount your underlying loan to the seller or move it to another property you own, so you receive all the cash yourself. This process is called substitution of collateral and was discussed earlier in this chapter.

I know that all this fancy talk about seller financing will not sink in the first time to some of you, but don't worry. The more you study and do, the easier it becomes. If the third offer stumps you, just ignore it and work on the first or second options. Either one can make several thousand dollars for you within a few days.

SCENARIO 2: **Answers**

Offer 1: ($20,000) $8,000 cash and assume the $12,000 mortgage.

Offer 2: ($23,000) $3,000 down, assume $12,000 mortgage, and give a second for $8,000, all due within six months, no payments, and no interest.

For both the above offers, re-read the Scenario 1 answers and apply the same solutions. The only difference is that you're assuming a loan for part of the purchase price instead of paying it off with cash.

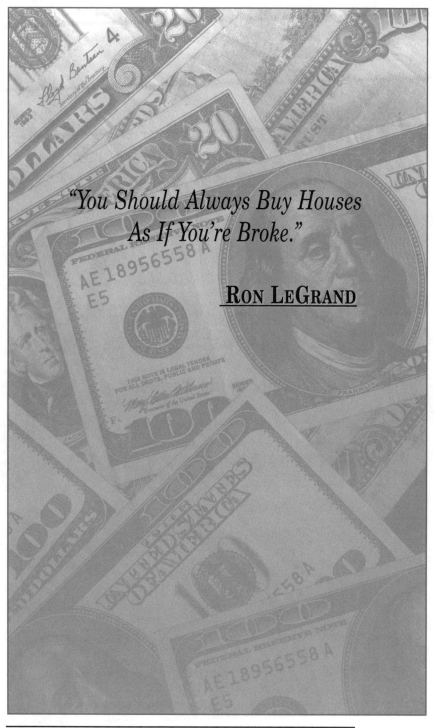

*"You Should Always Buy Houses
As If You're Broke."*

RON LeGRAND

*The best executive is the one who
has sense enough to pick good men
to do what he wants done,
and self-restraint enough to keep
from meddling with them
while they do it.*

*Our chief want in life is sombody
who will make us do what we can.*

Ralph Waldo Emerson

Chapter

Land Trusts
and Legal
Considerations

Are you aware that every time you sign your name on a note, you're risking everything you own to fulfill that debt? Did you know that in most states creditors can sue for default on a mortgage note and come after you personally without even bothering with the house? That's their right. They can look to all your other assets to satisfy your debt in place of, or in addition to, the property you mortgaged.

But don't worry! I have a solution to that problem for some types of financing. This solution also solves several other problems associated with owning real estate. It is simple, yet it is extremely important to all of us who buy houses. Anyone can use it, and it doesn't cost a nickel extra to take advantage of it. This solution is called a "land trust." First, let's learn what it is. Then we'll do a crash course on why and how to use it.

DEFINITION OF A LAND TRUST

It's irrelevant to us, as investors, how the land trust came about, or that there's a lot of history behind it. Such trusts were first used hundreds of years ago, but we only need to focus on how they can benefit us now. For simplicity, consider the land trust a method of taking title to property, nothing more, nothing less.

It is an agreement between the officer of the trust, called the "trustee," and the person who really controls the property. That person is called the "beneficiary." The trust identifies certain duties that each agrees to perform. The agreement is signed by both parties, and then it becomes the property of the beneficiary, with the trustee sometimes retaining a copy. The beneficiary owns the trust, and the trust owns the property. The trustee has only those powers granted to him or her by the beneficiary, and he or she performs minimal duties — usually just signing the documents. The trustee has no personal liability or responsibility to do anything more than those minimal tasks.

REASONS TO USE A LAND TRUST

Savvy investors use land trusts every day. This powerful document offers personal and legal advantages not associated with any other kind of property ownership. First, I'll list the benefits and then we'll discuss each briefly.

PRIVACY

Secrecy is an important aspect of a trust. Nobody knows you are the beneficiary, except for you, the trustee, and your closing agent. When somebody checks the title to the property, you don't own the property. In fact, you have no interest in the property as far as the rest of the world knows. All they see is that the property is owned by a trust. They do not know the beneficiary's name. The only way they will find that out is by court order, or if your trustee has a big mouth.

A deed is recorded at the courthouse. It bears the name of the trustee as grantee. Nowhere does it mention the beneficiary's name. The trust document, itself, remains in the possession of the beneficiary. It isn't recorded anywhere, nor does it become public knowledge. Therefore, you have total privacy.

LOAN LIABILITY

In the absence of a due-on-sale clause, the trust can be used to eliminate personal liability totally. Most FHA loans closed prior to December 15, 1989, and all VA loans closed prior to

March 1, 1988, do not contain due-on-sale clauses. Therefore, they require no qualifying to assume. So, the trust as a legal entity can assume those loans, thus foregoing the need for you to assume them personally. If, in fact, the trust can assume the loan, then why would you ever want to do it personally? The answer is, of course, you never would. This move keeps the loan off your credit report and your financial statement. You assume no liability for the debt. By the way, it costs no more to handle things the right way.

The trust can and should be used to create seller carryback financing. There is absolutely no reason for you to ever personally sign a note to a seller. If you don't heed this advice, you may very well be headed for an expensive real world seminar.

The process really is simple. The trust takes title to the house, so the trustee signs the note as trustee. Your name appears nowhere on the document. Therefore, you are not personally liable. As long as the words "as trustee" appear after the trustee's signature, he or she is not liable, either. Presto! You have just created a note that won't ever come back to haunt you.

LAWSUIT PROTECTION

Another key reason to use a land trust is lawsuit protection. It is not a foolproof plan to keep you from getting sued, because your beneficial interest can be attached. However, it is a lot better than owning property in your own name. The first thing an attorney will do in preparation for suing you is check your assets. All he can do is check your name. If your name doesn't show up, and it won't, he does not have a clue that you have anything to do with this property.

The only way he can find out is to get wind that you own properties in trust, call you in for a deposition, and ask you point blank, "Do you own any interest in any trusts?" At that time, you have to either answer yes, or commit perjury.

Let's assume, however, that you leave your properties titled in your own name, or even worse, jointly with your spouse. Now, you get sued, and the plaintiff is awarded a large judgment over and above your insurance benefits. The minute that judgment is recorded, it attaches to your properties and prevents any future sale or refinancing until the judgment is satisfied, if ever. In fact, the plaintiff can now start action to attach your assets, and everything you worked for is lost.

On the other hand, let's say your properties were in a land trust before the action started. First of all, a name search will produce nothing because you own nothing, as far as the public records are concerned.

This alone will stop most lawsuits in their tracks. If it is obvious a judgment can't be collected if won, it would be fruitless to pursue a lawsuit and incur the costs unless insurance proceeds were available. Under those circumstances, the case usually would be settled out of court.

But let's assume none of that happens, you get sued anyway, and they get a judgment. It doesn't attach to the properties because you don't own them. The trust owns the house, and you own the trust.

Before we get too smug, be aware this does not prevent a good attorney from coming after your interest in the trust. But first, he must discover you have an interest; and, second, someone must be willing to pay the high costs of another separate, expensive and risky lawsuit. While it's not a foolproof lawsuit protector, it sure beats owning property in your own name.

ESTATE PLANNING

A land trust is a good first step to estate planning, but it is by no means a total plan. Many kinds of trusts and other entities are available, but that's a subject I'll deal with in another book.

If your property is in a trust and you die, whoever is your beneficiary now owns this trust. Whatever interest you owned, he or she now owns.

However, to avoid probate, in most cases, this needs to be taken a step further. The most widely used method is to place the land trust in a living trust. Several courses on this subject are available.

EASE OF TRANSFER

When you sell to a buyer who understands trusts, quite often he or she would prefer you to assign him or her the trust, rather than having the trust deed the property to them. This action saves closing costs because nothing changes at the courthouse. The trust still owns the house and you are simply selling the trust. It is done with one sheet of paper called an "Assignment of Beneficial Interest." It's as simple as you signing it, your trustee signing it, and you handing it to the buyer. That's it! Now, of course, your buyer will want to check the title first, and will probably want someone to prepare a closing statement, but all the normal transfer and recording costs have been avoided.

BANK LOANS

When you go to a bank to borrow money that is secured by property, the bank will require your personal signature on the note. It will not let you take title in the trust because the bank doesn't understand it. If you have intentions of buying a property and refinancing, don't take title in the name of the trust. The bank will not make a loan to a trust. If you are going to refinance, take title in your name, refinance, and then place the property in a trust. The lender cannot call the loan due as long as you are the controlling interest in the trust, even if the loan contains a due-on-sale clause. In 1982, the Garn - St. Germain Federal Depository Institution Act made it illegal for a lender to call a loan simply because property has been transferred into a trust. If you experience a problem with a lender because of this point, write to me at my office, and I'll send you a copy of a letter you can mail them. It should stop them in their tracks.

APPOINTING A TRUSTEE

The trustee must be a person you trust. You could make a family member, friend, or title agent your trustee. The trustee can be someone out of state. But remember, the trustee does the signing for any transactions of the trust. The trustee can close deals for you when you are not in town because of the trust provisions. But the trustee can sign documents only because you, as beneficiary, give him permission. The beneficiary has all the control. The trustee has no control, except to do what the beneficiary tells him to do. The trustee signs all documents at the direction of the beneficiary.

Of course, a dishonest trustee can illegally sign away a deed to your property. Someone taking the deed should check with the beneficiary and even get something in writing from him that taking the deed is, in fact, in keeping with his wishes.

This has been a brief introduction to a few of the key ideas regarding the use of trusts. To really use trusts effectively, you need to learn much more, but it is too extensive a subject for this one book.

I have thousands of students using land trusts nationwide. That is because trusts are simple to use, cost nothing extra, and provide all the benefits previously discussed. Bearing that in mind, please don't let a so-called expert convince you otherwise. Get the facts from the people who know, instead of constantly reinventing the wheel.

If you buy real estate, you should be using land trusts! It's just that simple.

AVOIDING TITLE PROBLEMS

Never, repeat, NEVER buy a property without a thorough title check and title insurance. You need the title insurance, in addition to the thorough title check, because no title check can be declared absolutely perfect and complete. A long list of things can go wrong with a title, such as unrecorded documents and forged signatures. Even the best title company can't know everything.

You must order a title check as soon as you put a property under contract. You can't do anything with a property unless it has a good title. Always ask the title insurance company for a written title insurance commitment as soon as you close a deal. It is also wise to evaluate your title insurance company's strength and ability to pay out in the event of a title problem. A number of title insurance companies have failed in recent years.

Section VI
Success

Opportunity...often it comes in the form of misfortune, or temporary defeat.

Napoleon Hill

Selling Houses Fast

SELLING RETAIL

It's easy to buy houses at a good price when you know how to do it. But Quick-Turning a house to a retail buyer takes a little more effort. Remember, you don't receive your profit until the property is sold. Even if you refinance, the financing has to be repaid.

Quite frankly, marketing houses to an owner/occupant who qualifies for a loan is the hardest part of our business and the weakest link. But it's also the most profitable method on a per-house basis. Before we go any further, let me point out again it is not mandatory that you get into the retail business. In fact, you shouldn't, unless you have the funds, have access to them, or become skilled at optioning houses so you don't need funds. If you're weak on these points, perhaps you should stick with wholesaling and/or assumptions.

So how do you market a house and sell it fast? After all, you want your money as soon as possible!

PLANNING YOUR TOTAL SALES STRATEGY

If you're buying low to sell high, you're always looking for customers who can qualify for a loan. A house will have to look nice after repairs to attract this kind of buyer. Give buyers a reason to buy your house. Keep in mind you're not going to live in this house; you're only fixing it up to market it.

You will want to do good-quality, but not expensive, repairs. Resist the temptation to spend a lot of unnecessary money. Adding a little wallpaper, paneling, ceiling fans, and so forth, is all it takes to make the property look nice and livable. Don't cheat on repairs, or you could end up having a house on the market for a long time. At the same time, remember this is only inventory and doesn't require the best available materials or craftsmanship.

The whole repair process doesn't take long. The average house takes from two or three days to two or three weeks to completely rehab, depending on the extent of the work, if you use a contractor who has one or two men working with him. Don't over complicate this process. Keep it simple, straightforward, and fast.

The biggest mistake some of my students make is to do the repairs themselves. In my opinion, this is a gross waste of their time. Do you want to get paid as a handyman or as an investor? The answer is investor! The pay is higher, MUCH HIGHER! While you're spending time trying to save a dollar, you're losing $10 in profits. To make this really simple, let me put it another way: we don't do repairs — we write checks!

These basic things must be done to sell a house:

First, the house must be ready to market. It must be in good repair, and the work must be good quality. Act as though it's a buyer's market, whether it is or not. You're trying to attract a buyer who has good credit, so the house must be a cut above the others on the market. After all, buyers who have good credit have the maximum choice available to them in the marketplace. A failure to get the house ready will cost you dearly in the long run, due to holding costs.

Second, plan the whole process ahead of time. Always know what you're going to do with a property before you buy it. Know the way out before you go in. Don't permit yourself to become overloaded with too many properties to sell at the same time. Take care of the first property before moving on to the next.

Plan with the calendar in mind, as well. For example, December may be the worst time of year to sell a house.

Third, you need to know how, when and where you're going to advertise this property. Know which publications you'll use to place ads, the type of ads you'll run, and, most importantly, how you're going to follow up on the calls that come in because of the ads. You'll need a system to handle these calls as they arrive. Prepare a Buyer's Fact Sheet (see Appendix H) for all the calls you receive. Take advantage of them by collecting information about prospective buyers for future use.

When you become adept at gathering buyer information, you'll soon learn to find houses to suit their needs. When you figure this out, selling becomes a cinch.

Fourth, decide which lender you want to be involved. When you need a new FHA, VA or conventional loan on the house, make sure you know who is going to provide that financing. You need to know the interest rates and closing costs. Have a lender in mind ahead of time for your prospective buyer so the loan process will get under way as soon as you have the house under contract. The buyer will want to know how much his payments will be. You should know all of this even before you put the ad in the newspaper.

Fifth, if you use seller financing, play with the numbers before you get the calls. You need to be fully prepared at the time possible buyers respond, or you will lose many opportunities to make the sale. When they call and ask the questions, you need to know all the answers. You only get one shot at them.

REPAIR TIPS

Preparing a house to market is an area where a lot of investors fail. They don't do the repairs properly. The house needs to be in tip-top shape. But I don't fix them up as though I'm going to live in them!

I work on the exterior first. When a buyer drives up, a nice exterior will make him want to look at the interior. Most landscaping money should be spent on the front of the house. I recommend flowers, wood chips, mulch, or anything else that looks nice. If you don't know how to landscape, you can hire someone to do it correctly and inexpensively. In most cases, you shouldn't spend more than $200 to $300 to make the front of a house look presentable.

I use semigloss paint, in two colors, to make the exterior of the house stand out: light blue and a darker blue trim, or light gray with a darker gray trim. Either is quite attractive. I then accent the front with shutters and a fancy front door in burgundy. I give extra care to the front windows because they affect the entire look of the house.

I don't install expensive cabinets in the kitchen since pressboard cabinets are adequate. Redoing a kitchen completely shouldn't cost more than $1,000 to $1,500. I install a double sink with new faucets, but I don't spend a lot of money on appliances, since they're not needed to sell the house.

If you doubt you can remodel a kitchen for this price, as I suspect you do, I suggest you take a trip to your nearest Home Depot, Builders Supply, or other home repair store. Look around and price a whole kitchen containing a sink-base cabinet, counter top, sink, faucet, trap, and three or four upper cabinets. You'll be shocked to learn the whole works, with really nice cabinets, can be purchased for $700 to $800.

While you're in the store, search for other items that can make a house look nice that don't cost much. You'll discover it's the little things that sell a house. For example, I do whatever I can to keep the house smelling nice, like hanging a cinnamon deodorizer. Small items such as fancy electric plug covers are cheap and make the house look richer. Using wallpaper with borders makes a kitchen and bath stand out. I put ceiling fans in just about every room of a house. They cost only $40 to $50 each and really help make the sale. Total cost for fans usually runs about $200 to $300 installed.

I hang mini-blinds on all the windows for an average cost of about $10.00 per window. If you can't find ready-made mini-blinds that fit, you can have them made to order. If they cost about $10 a window and you have 20 windows, the cost will be approximately $200. If the house is sitting vacant for two weeks or longer because it doesn't have mini-blinds, and your mortgage payment is $400 a month, $200 is money well spent. I don't put curtains in a house because I have had better results by only adding mini-blinds. Generally, I use a color other than white to give the house more warmth.

Here are some more tips that will make a house sell faster. In the living room, I use bright paneling, but not on every wall. Sometimes it's even more effective to panel half and paper the rest. I use molding in the living room, family room and dining room, but I don't use expensive molding unless I'm dealing with a more expensive house.

I almost always carpet my houses with earth tones or solid colors, and I'm careful to avoid gaudy colors. I seldom spend more than $10 a yard total for carpet, pad and installation, with the carpet alone costing about $6 or $7 a yard.

In the bathroom, I usually redo the bathtub at a cost of about $100 to $300. This cost covers professional bathtub refinishing, which gives a better-than-new look. Using this method, I have found it's rarely necessary to replace the tub, and less expensive, too. When a wall can't be fixed with paper or paint, I just put marolite over it. Marolite is a printed or patterned paneling designed for damp areas such as bathrooms. It's also good behind a range in the kitchen. If the toilet has stains that won't come out, I put denture tablets in it. These clean the toilet very well, especially if you use about six or eight tablets and make sure the water level is above the stain. If the toilet is not salvageable, replacement cost is about $70.

In the bedrooms, I use semigloss on the walls, and I paint the trim a couple of shades darker, again avoiding gaudy colors. I do not have my workmen strip the wood and restain it, since this would be too much work and generally not worth the effort.

Some other important things I do, and others that I don't, are worth mentioning here. For example, I almost always add central heat and air before I market a house. You might not think this is necessary on some houses, especially the cheap ones, but just remember that I'm the guy who has done this more than 1,000 times. I know beyond a shadow of a doubt that houses with CH&A sell faster than those without it. Just ask yourself which you'd rather buy. Your cost for installing a whole system from scratch on a 1,200-square-foot house should not exceed $2,500 total. This, of course, assumes you hire the right people to do the job.

Before you insist that this can't be done for that price in your area, or that I'm full of hot air, just remember: I've been in cities all over the country, and I have successful students in most of them. Everywhere I go, I'm told this can't be done in the area. So when I hear those words, I simply point the skeptics to a student who has done it recently and let that student do the convincing. I've bought hundreds of CH&A systems and, believe me, it can be done and is done for that price on a regular basis. The trick is to hire a one- or two-man crew, one that has little or no overhead and that specializes in heat and air. Don't call the guys with the big, yellow-page ads.

Another important item most investors overlook is the roof. The tendency is to ignore the roof if it's borderline, and try to find a buyer who will ignore it as well. Forget it! Replace the roof in the beginning and see how much faster the house will sell.

If you ignore these two items just mentioned, roof and CH&A, be prepared for a hard lesson as some investors have learned. I know, I was one of them. Do the repairs the right way, and you will end up with more profit. Incidentally, when you add these two items, you are increasing the value of the house by several thousand dollars. More importantly, you are increasing the saleability.

THE SMART WAY TO USE A REALTOR®

When I'm using a REALTOR® to market my property, I get an "exclusive agency listing." That gives the REALTOR® the right to market the property, and I agree that that REALTOR® is the only one I will hire. However, it also gives me the right to market the property at the same time, without paying the

REALTOR® a fee if I find the buyer. Although a great many brokers will not enter into this type of agreement, you can always find one who will, and who is capable of making the sale. As an alternative, though, you could enter into a regular agreement and just add a buy-out clause. That's a clause that states that, if you find a buyer on your own, you will buy the REALTOR® out of the contract for $500, or any other mutually negotiated amount.

A REALTOR® will want a six-month contract with no contingencies, but you don't have to agree to that! Never give a REALTOR® more than a 90-day agreement. You can always extend the agreement if you feel the sales job has been adequate. If you're concerned the house may not be advertised properly, negotiate a lower commission and place the ads yourself, or pay for the ads your REALTOR® runs. That way, you know the house will stay in front of the public, and your REALTOR® won't have the cost or the risk of the ads.

SELLING THE HOUSE YOURSELF

As soon as the exterior is finished, I recommend putting up a "FOR SALE" sign. Don't use a sign that looks too professional. A simple "FOR SALE BY OWNER" sign with a phone number will get just as many, if not more, calls than will a fancy, expensive sign. Of course, the sign should be easily visible.

When you send a person to look at a house, it's good practice to fill out a "Telephone Questionnaire for Potential Buyers," also known as the "Buyer's Fact Sheet." In doing this, you are "qualifying the buyer," and the process will separate the tire kickers and the would-be buyers from the real customers who have real cash or credit. A few minutes on the phone will save you a lot of gasoline and time.

If this house is not what they want, you might be able to find a property more suited to them. This is one way to have a buyer before you buy your next property. You know what they're looking for, what size payments they can afford, where they want to live, how much money they have to put down, and whether they can qualify for a loan.

Here's an example of qualifying a possible buyer:

Q. "Do you want to look at the house alone, or would you prefer I meet you there?"

A. "We would like to meet at the house, Ron."

Q. "Let me ask you a question. I have advertised the price for this house in the paper as $50,000, and it's going to require a new loan. Do you feel you can qualify for a new loan?"

A. "Probably not."

Q. "I'll have to get a little information from you. It looks like this one's not going to work for you, but maybe I can find you another one that will. Do you have a minute to give me some answers to a few questions?"

I didn't need to show him this house because I found out he didn't qualify. I would, at this point, ask him a few questions. If I feel he is capable of buying, I would go find him a house based on what he has told me. It would have to be one that wouldn't require new financing where the financing could be assumed without qualifying — the same type of house I discussed in the chapter on assumptions.

If he is qualified for a loan but doesn't have much down payment he is valuable, but obviously not as valuable to us as someone with a lot of cash. The qualified buyer who has good credit, can qualify for a loan, and who has the down payment can have his pick of any house on the market today. This is the kind of buyer everyone is seeking. When you have a pile of fact sheets on potential buyers for your properties, you will be able to match a house you want to sell for all cash with someone who has the credit, down payment, and desire for that type of house in that particular location.

RUNNING ADS

The first thing to be determined about your ad is where you are going to run it. You can advertise in the leading newspaper, the weeklies, and the neighborhood publications. When running an ad, be sure to check out the contract rates, which are often substantially lower if you agree to run some sort of ad each week. You can save about 25%.

Of course, the point of running an ad is to get prospective buyers to call about it, or you're not going to sell the house. I recommend avoiding the use of too many abbreviations because things that may seem obvious to you may not be easily understood by your prospects. Do you understand this one?

"Westside, 3/2, 2C/G, A/P Large D/R and F/R, CH/A, $75,000 Call 999-9999"

In different parts of the country, abbreviations mean different things. You may still be trying to figure out what all that code means, but believe it or not, I've seen ads even more difficult to decipher than this one.

If you wanted a prospect to understand the above ad, it should have been written more along the lines of

"Westside, 3/2, A/ground pool, 2 Car Gar, large dining and family room, Cent. heat and air $75,000, Owner will help. 555-5555."

What do I mean by "Owner will help?" That's just a phrase I use to get people to call me instead of calling another guy's ad. When people ask what it means, I simply ask in turn, "What kind of help do you need?"

If they don't have enough down payment, I'll suggest some of the ways I can help them get it, as I'll discuss shortly. If they feel their credit is weak, I'll find out why and see if there is a way I can help them overcome any small problems. I frequently get people approved for loans, where others fail to, because I take the time to assist them with things like writing explanation letters, getting old derogatory items removed from their credit reports, or showing them how to restructure their debt so their debt ratio falls in line.

If I see I can't get them a loan because of poor credit, the next thing I want to know is how much they can put down. Quite often, buyers have several thousand dollars for a down payment. If so, I'll shift them to another deal where I can put them in an assumable, no-qualifying house. If that's not possible, I'll keep their Buyer's Information Sheet on hand until I find a house on which we can deal, then give them a call.

If the monthly payment is too high for them I'll suggest a lower, adjustable-rate loan or help them into a less expensive house. If I'm going to spend the money to run the ad, I certainly want to exhaust all angles before giving up on a good prospect.

RESPONDING TO CALLS

If you've done a good job writing and placing an ad, you'll receive a lot of calls. Don't use an answering machine! About 50% of the people calling will not leave a message on a machine. The next best thing, if you can't answer the phone yourself, is to hire a live answering service. They're not expensive and they make it hard for a caller to hang up.

Get the caller's name, address and phone number, and find out what they're looking for. You can build a buyer's list this way. The point is to get as much information as possible from people who call about a particular house you've advertised.

Even if they don't qualify for what you're currently selling, you can always look for something else that will suit them.

Don't over sell! Just give callers the pertinent information. Answer only the questions they ask. Don't rattle on about the house. You can give them the address, so they can go see the house from the outside, then make an appointment to show them the inside. This is preferred to your going with them on their first visit. (Of course, you will have left the blinds open so anyone looking at the house can see inside.)

When they call back to make an appointment to see the inside of the house, it's time to prequalify them. That conversation may go something like this:

"Hi, Ron, I went by your house the other day. I'd like to take a look at the inside."

"Great, Mr. Buyer. When would you like to do this?"

"9 o'clock, Thursday."

"9 o'clock, Thursday, OK. Can I answer any questions before I meet you out there, Mr. Buyer?"

"No, Ron, we can talk when I meet you."

"Let me ask you this, Mr. Buyer. How did you plan to finance the house, assuming that you like the inside?"

"We were hoping that you could help us out with that, Ron."

"What kind of help do you need?"

"I'll probably need some help with some of the closing costs."

OK. We'll talk about that when we get there. In other words, Mr. Buyer, you are going to want new financing?"

"Right."

"Mr. Buyer, you understand that the property is going to require about $3,000 down. Is that a problem?"

"Just $3,000 flat? No closing costs?"

"Well, closing costs are usually split by the buyer and the seller, Mr. Buyer. Are closing costs going to be a problem for you?"

"I can only come up with $3,000."

"We can work with that."

"Good."

"OK. How's your credit?"

"Well, it's been pretty good for the last couple of years."

"About the only other thing I can think of, Mr. Buyer, that would stop you from getting the loan is if your debt ratio doesn't work out. Do you think you're overloaded with debts?"

"Well, I just bought a car."
"What's your gross income, Mr. Buyer?"

"It depends on if it rains, or not. I can't work all the time. I've got $xxx"
"Are you steadily employed, Mr. Buyer?"

"Yes, if it doesn't rain, I can go out and work."
"Can you prove your income, Mr. Buyer?"

"I'm sort of self-employed right now, Ron."
"Can you prove your income?"

"Well I haven't been employed for over a year."
"Are you saying that you can't prove your income for this year, Mr. Buyer?"

"Well I can for the last couple of years. I was employed by someone else."
"Mr. Buyer, can you give me a profit and loss statement for this year showing that you made some money?"

(silence)

"Have you made any money this year, Mr. Buyer?"
"Thanks, Ron."

If the buyer hangs up at this point, it's a blessing, because I have saved myself a trip. On the other hand, if the caller answers all my questions with a yes, I know that I may have a qualified buyer. I would then be willing to show the property. But if the caller can't prove his income, there is no reason to waste time running out there. The exception would be if I'm selling a no-qualifying assumption deal. In that case, the only thing I need to know is whether he has the money.

The key questions you must ask are:

How's their credit? Is it going to be a problem?

Do they actually have the down payment now? Are the funds in the bank now?

Do they feel they are overloaded with debt? What is their income to debt ratio?

Do they have steady, verifiable income?

The above information must be obtained to prequalify the buyer. You should get answers to those questions after the buyer looks at the outside of the house, by himself, and before he gets to see the inside.

As soon as the lender takes the application, a request for verification of funds will be sent to the buyer's bank to make sure the money is really there. If it's not, the loan will not progress until the money is in the buyer's account. This explains why you should ask the question, "Are the funds in the bank now?"

In some cases, a gift letter can be used. That means the buyer can receive a gift from a relative for the down payment. He or she can't borrow the money for the down payment, but money can be given to him using a gift letter. Lenders allow relatives only to give such money, not sellers. In the case of some bank loans, anyone except the seller can gift the funds.

Call your buyer weekly and check with the lender often. Communicate with him, find out what is happening, and keep on top of the situation. Try to solve problems before they become unsolvable.

Two often-forgotten items must be watched by you. **First**, the buyer will need a prepaid insurance policy for one year in advance at closing. Tell the buyer that when you get the contract.

Second, you as the seller shouldn't forget to obtain the pay-off letters on the underlying loans. If you wait until the last minute, the closing could be delayed. Most likely, the deal will not close without the payoff letters, so be sure to remember them. You as the seller should take control and make sure all the documents needed to close are obtained in a timely manner. Failure to do so will delay both the closing and the day you'll be able to put your profits in your pocket.

ADDING CREATIVITY TO ACTION

One of the easiest ways to stand heads above the competition in the house business is to show a little creativity in your marketing. Be different! More people will call about your ad, you'll make more profit, and you'll sell houses faster. Here are some ideas and examples of ways to put more cash in your pocket.

First of all, remember that even if you have a nice house in a nice neighborhood, you still may have trouble selling it. Always have at least two different ways to sell the property, if possible. The number of creative selling techniques is limited only by your imagination. The ones I prefer to use include:

- Split funding the down payment
- Eliminating the down payment altogether through trading
- Seller financing the deal

Let's discuss each of these techniques. Remember, these are not the only ones that work — they are just my favorites. When you have mastered these, you'll be able to sell your houses faster than ever before!

SPLIT FUNDING THE DOWN PAYMENT

Making the down payment smaller for the buyer can be accomplished in several ways. One of the simplest is to split it into two or more parts. Think of it as taking the down payment in installments. For example, if you want a $5,000 down payment and the buyer has only $2,000, put the buyer in the house and let him pay you $500 a month extra, in addition to the regular payments, until the down payment is paid. Anything you and the buyer can agree on will work. It depends on the individual situation. Of course, the downside to this method is that it could take months for the sale to go through, while you wait for your buyer to raise the money. This method works only if you can wait.

ELIMINATING THE DOWN PAYMENT

Eliminating the need for a cash down payment altogether is the next basic method to use when selling your property. How do you do this and still make money? Trade! In essence, you look for something you value more than someone else does, and take it for the down payment. If you're willing to take something on trade, put this in your ad:

"I will take anything on trade for down payment. Car, truck, motor home, mobile home, horses, stock, etc."

You can also receive other real estate in exchange for the down payment. Don't lose sight of the fact that you won't have a house that fits every caller's needs. So what do you do with the potential good buyers who, for one reason or another, can't or won't buy one of your houses? Make money, of course!

Fill out a fact sheet about them and contact other investors to see if they have anything. If they do, give the investor the person's name and fact sheet in exchange for a previously negotiated fee, payable if the deal closes. Shared listings of potential buyers are mutually profitable. However, if you find a good qualified buyer with good credit, cash, or both, I suggest you get busy and find them a house. Buyers are harder to find than good deals on houses. Don't waste them!

SELLER FINANCING THE DEAL

The next technique is really a whole set of methods that make it easier for the buyer to buy, yet keep the deal profitable for you. That technique is seller financing.

Seller financing has three advantages when used to market your property.

First, it gets the attention of the buyer and sets your house apart from other properties in the marketplace.

Second, it makes it easier for the purchaser to buy your house.

Third, it's highly profitable! Over the life of a loan, you often can double or triple the profit you would otherwise make. The following is just a brief introduction into selling with seller financing.

FINANCE COMPANIES, YOUR ACE IN THE HOLE

Any property you own can be owner financed, but your objective should be to get your cash back, not leave it buried in the property. A buyer may not be able to qualify for a loan for the full purchase price. Nevertheless, you can hold a second mortgage and get the buyer a loan for 50%, 60% or 75% LTV from a finance company.

There are finance companies in every major city who will make these lower LTV loans to buyers who simply can't qualify for bank loans or government financing. You'll be shocked at the bad credit some of them will accept. I suggest that you hit the bricks and talk to five or six finance companies, such as Beneficial Finance or ITT, to learn their loan requirements.

It will make your sales job much easier if you buy the property correctly to begin with, so you don't have to cash out at 100% of the sale price to make a profit. The goal is to get whatever cash down payment you can, get the buyer a loan for a percentage of the sale price, and take back a second mortgage. You can keep the second or sell it for quick cash, if you can find a buyer. This could be a better deal for some sellers than all cash. I personally prefer to have all my investment, and then some, out of the property when I do this, so all my paper profit is free.

The downside to using finance companies is that the rates are high, so the payments are high as well. Therefore, this will work only on lower-cost houses — those priced under $60,000. A 75% LTV loan on a $60,000 house is $45,000. Amortized over

15 years at 13%, the payment would be $569 per month, plus whatever you and the buyer can agree on about the second-mortgage payment you are carrying back. Even though this is still a tolerable payment to a semi-qualified buyer, it is high. It's obvious that the higher the price, the higher the mortgage, but it's still a method worth exploring for several reasons:

1. These loans require minimal qualifying.
2. You get an answer in about 48 hours.
3. These loans usually close in two weeks or less.
4. They have low closing costs and little lender scrutiny.
5. The lender requires little or no down payment.

TRADING THE PAPER

At some point, you're going to wonder what can be done with all those small second mortgages. You can use them to trade for other property. So you find a seller who will take several second mortgages you own for his equity, instead of giving him back a mortgage on the house you're buying. You can buy a property free and clear if you have enough second mortgages to use for trade. The person from whom you are buying the house will take four, five, six or more of these little second mortgages in exchange for his property. Then, he collects the payments from all of them.

Or, if you want to do something really dumb, you can trade them for toys, as I once did. I swapped $30,000 worth of seconds for a free-and-clear motor home worth $30,000. I had run an ad in the paper stating I would trade some real estate for such a vehicle. A man called to say he had a motor home, and wanted to know what I had. After some conversation, I discovered what he really wanted was cash flow, not real estate, so I got the idea to trade five little second mortgages I owned.

My total incoming payments were $450 per month. His motor home was just sitting around, not being used, because his wife didn't want to leave town. We made the swap, and now I'm out $450 per month income and I have a motor home sitting around not being used! Maybe one day, if I keep begging, my wife will let me sell or trade it for something useful before it becomes worthless.

SELLING ON A WRAP

Another highly effective method I've used to finance properties is the wraparound mortgage. A wraparound is a single mortgage, created by a seller, that wraps around all the underlying mortgages.

For example, if you make a $50,000 sale and take $5,000 as the down payment, and there happens to be an existing $20,000 first mortgage and a $10,000 second mortgage, you can take back a $45,000 mortgage wrapped around the two underlying loans.

The buyer pays you $450 a month on the $45,000, and you pay $300 a month on your underlying payments. You get $150 per month cash flow and a $15,000 equity position in the note. You can then sell the paper for cash, but if you intend to sell wraparound mortgages, you have to become skilled at knowing the price for which you can sell them.

The process isn't complicated. The objective is to create the wraparound mortgage and sell it at a discount, if that's what you want to do. By doing that, you can make the house quite saleable, because the buyer doesn't have to qualify at the bank. In selling the wraparound mortgage, however, be aware that anytime you convert a note to cash, you will suffer a sharp discount because of the time value of money. Cash received in the future is worth far less than cash received today. The further away the due date, the bigger the discount.

The discount is calculated based on the monthly payment you are receiving, the number of payments still to be paid, the LTV ratio, and the buyer's credit. The higher the monthly payments being received for the mortgage, the less the discount you will take. It's just that simple.

However, if you have a buyer whose credit is very bad, you may not be able to sell the mortgage until it ages several years. Your buyer doesn't have to be perfect, but a real bum will make it difficult to convert your note to cash.

You don't have to sell off the whole mortgage. People who buy mortgages are looking for a cash flow that can be bought at a discount rate. The more quickly they get their money back, the more that cash flow is worth.

Don't worry about a due-on-sale clause on the underlying financing if you intend to sell off the wrap. If you are selling a wraparound mortgage to a traditional mortgage buyer, all the underlying mortgages are going to be paid off before you get paid. The note buyer will simply calculate the amount he or she would pay for the mortgage or trust deed as if it were a first mortgage and there were no underlying liens. When the funds are disbursed, all liens will be paid off, and you will get what remains, so the note buyer will then have a first mortgage or trust deed.

Here's an example: Suppose you are selling a house for $50,000. It's carrying a $20,000 loan with a due-on-sale clause, and it has a balloon payment due in three months. If you know you are going to sell this paper, you don't care about the clauses, because all the underlying loans are paid off as soon as the mortgage is sold. You can wrap it, knowing it is going to be paid off. You had better understand this type of deal well enough, however, to be absolutely sure the underlying loans are going to be paid off.

You should even go so far as to pre-approve that mortgage sale before you close the deal. Get an application, send it to a mortgage buyer with the terms of the note, and let him tell you what he will pay for it before you ever close.

SELLING WITH NOTHING DOWN

If you are feeling really generous and want to sell zero down, be prepared for your phone to ring off the hook! Just be sure to obtain additional collateral. Hold the title to something the buyer owns until some sort of down payment is received. On a zero-down deal, always make sure the buyer will lose something of value if he doesn't live up to the agreement. Additional collateral could come in several forms, but it is usually a mortgage on another property in addition to the one you're selling.

That way, if the buyer defaults, both properties are at risk. Of course, a lien could also be against non-realty things like cars, boats, mobile homes, or motor homes.

ADDING "BOOT," THE GRAVY ON THE DEAL

Another advantage of seller financing your property involves selling other personal property. For example, suppose you have a boat you'd like to sell. (From my experience, if you have a boat, you probably DO want to get rid of it.) You can add the value of the boat to that of the house and finance it with the purchase.

PERSONAL GUARANTEES FOR SELLER CARRYBACK

I strongly urge you to obtain a personal guarantee on all seller carryback notes when you sell. This puts you in a position, in most states, to come after the seller personally to collect the debt. That means you can sue on the note and not foreclose the mortgage, if you wish. Everything the buyer owns is at risk until your debt is paid.

When you get a judgment on such a note, you can attach everything belonging to the buyer. If it is not enough to cover the debt, you still can foreclose on the mortgage and sell the property. Can you see why a personal guarantee is a powerful motivator for your buyer to pay you? And do you understand why you should not guarantee notes personally, if at all possible?

The ideas expressed in this chapter on how to market your houses are just the beginning. Be creative. Get expert advice, so you are always safe, but do have some fun trying different ideas. As I said above, the creative selling techniques available to you are limited only by your imagination.

They say art is a good investment. Learning the fine art of creatively selling your houses will put more real cash in your pocket than you can imagine!

SELLING WHOLESALE

This is the easiest part of marketing houses. Everyone's looking for a bargain, so if you have the knowledge to find those bargains, you are very much in demand. Your objective is simply to locate and tie up a good deal, then quickly sell it to one of two kinds of buyers. Some are investors who like to make a Quick-Turn profit or acquire rentals. Others will be owner/occupants simply hunting a fixer-upper they can buy cheaply to repair and live in.

Let's see if we can't figure out some ways to attract these bargain hunters. First, I'll assume you have located a good deal on a junker, and the seller has given you a signed purchase and sale agreement. Now you're faced with the task of either raising the money yourself to buy it, or selling it before you have to close the purchase. Let's say you found a HUD repo worth $50,000, after repairs, that needs about $7,000 in work. Your offer of $17,000 cash was accepted. The problem is you don't have $17,000 in cash. You decide you want to wholesale the house for $20,000 and let someone else worry about it. All you want is your $3,000 profit and a clean break. You don't want to bother with fixing the house or finding a qualified buyer. Once you have a signed contract to purchase, you have the right to begin the sale. So you run an ad in the paper that says:

"Handyman special, cheap, cash, 999-9999."

This ad doesn't look like much, but it will produce calls from all kinds of buyers, investors, and owner/occupants. The trick is to make full use of all the calls that come in. Most people would ramble on and try to convince the caller this is a really great deal. Then they would ask the caller to go see the house. That's where it would end, unless the caller called back and showed interest.

But since we paid for the ad, we're going to make the best use of it and build ourselves a buyer's list. This list will contain the name, phone number, and qualifying data about every caller. It will be a record of what they want, where they want it, whether they have cash, and whether they are an investor or occupant. It will have other pertinent information, as well.

My friend, this list could be your most valuable asset. It will be your lifeblood and source of ready money. It will soon become your customer list. It's just as important to you as a doctor's list of patients or an insurance agent's list of clients.

But once you build this list, which will take all of a few days to do, then you will develop a new problem: finding enough deals to supply all the buyers!

That's right. Soon you will be able to spend your time looking for good deals to wholesale instead of looking for buyers, because you'll have more demand than you can supply. All from running an ad to attract the right people, and then collecting that information instead of wasting it.

Soon you will be experiencing the pleasure of taking a call from a prospective long-term customer, rather than from a short-term, one-time buyer. A slight change in your attitude about those incoming calls could mean the difference between a mediocre existence and the creation of more income than you can spend.

Let's assume you find only three deals a month as a full-time investor. Once you learn the ropes, this should mean you're making about 20 to 30 offers a month. If you're not getting those results, you're not doing the right things. The truth is I usually have a higher success ratio than that, but I'll allow you some time to get up to speed.

Let's also assume you wholesale all three deals and make only $5,000 per house. Now, the way I figure it, that's $15,000 a month without ever buying a house, doing repairs, borrowing money, qualifying buyers, making payments, or dealing with tenants.

You paid no franchise fee, took no risks, worked short hours, and had no employees. The best part is that you can begin immediately and start to profit soon after.

All of a sudden your buyer's list becomes a very important part of your life, doesn't it? Of course, this is assuming you take the time and spend the money necessary to get the proper training to make it all possible. But as my students across America have proven, success will come if you make the right offers on the right houses, then handle your deals the right way.

ASSUMPTIONS

Dealing in assumptions is a different world than wholesaling houses. In fact, it's on the opposite end of the spectrum. Instead of buying junkers at low wholesale prices, you're looking for nice houses in good, upscale areas. In addition, your buyer's market is owner/occupants only.

To refresh your memory, your objective is to finance a property and pass it along to your buyer without dealing with banks. Your profit will come from the difference between the amount you can collect as a down payment from your buyer and the amount of down payment you have to make to your seller.

What makes these houses easy to market is the buyer doesn't need good credit to qualify. If he or she has enough down payment to suit you, the buyer is qualified. Such buyers tend to be much less picky than qualified buyers, and they're much easier to work with. If you provide them with a nice house, in a nice area, with a reasonable down and monthly payments, you should have an easy sale. In fact, these houses are usually sold before I find them.

This is where I make good use of my buyer's list of people who have several thousand in cash, but who don't qualify for a traditional loan.

It's just a matter of showing the house to everyone on the list until one of them says yes. The process begins just as soon as I get a house under contract. So, by the time I am forced to close on my purchase, I have a buyer lined up, ready to buy. Most of the time, I'll simply have my seller deed directly to my buyer and leave with a check for the difference. This happens frequently when I've assumed an existing, no-qualifying loan that constitutes most of my purchase price, and the seller is getting very little or no cash.

If I'm creating a no-qualifying loan by giving the seller back a mortgage or trust deed, I'll almost always have to close first and then resell, even if only a few minutes later.

Remember, a no-qualifying loan is simply one that does not have a due-on-sale clause that would allow the lender to call the loan due on transfer. Don't forget that I'm taking title in a land trust and having the trust either assume the existing, no-qualifying loan or create the seller carryback note. I'll never become personally liable, and neither should you. If you choose to ignore this suggestion, you are likely to be headed for a very expensive seminar.

Now that we know what we're trying to accomplish, let's discuss how to find these buyers. Actually, it's quite easy. Just run an ad something like this: **"Northside, 3/2, No Qualifying, Low Down, $693 mo, 999-9999."** This little ad should produce tons of calls because of the words "no qualifying" and "low down."

If you create a buyer's list in the way we've previously discussed, you'll soon have a stack of good prospects. When potential buyers call and you have captured the information you want, then give them the address and let them look at the property from the outside. Ask them to call you back and let you know if they like the house so you can make an appointment to show them the inside. Of course, if the house is vacant, leave the shades open so they can look inside. Tell them it's OK to do just that.

When a potential customer, one who has seen the exterior and looked inside, calls you back, chances are excellent he is a genuine buyer. Now's the time to make an appointment to meet him, and his checkbook, and get a written contract signed and an earnest money deposit.

Remember, both the husband and wife must be present when you show the house. You can ask in plain terms:

"Will your wife be present when we meet?"
"No. She can't make it then."

"Let's reschedule a time when you both can be present."
"I don't see why she needs to be there, she always goes along with whatever I say anyway."

"I understand, but in order for me to take the house off the market if you like it, I'll need an OK from both of you. Is that going to present a problem?"
"No, I guess not."

"Good, I'll see you both there at 5:00 p.m. By the way, be sure to bring your checkbook. I'll need a deposit if this is the house you want."
"I don't know for sure I want the house yet."

"I understand. But if it is the one you want, I'll need a deposit to insure you get it, and I don't want to see you have to make another trip. I've had a lot of interest in the house, and the first person with a deposit wins. I'm only suggesting you come prepared."

When you have a nice house in a nice area and can offer great financing, you don't have to beg people to buy. These kinds of houses don't hang around long. There are too many people ready, willing and able to pounce on them as soon as they become available.

There are many variations of the assumption technique, such as selling on a wraparound mortgage and creating monthly cash flow, or selling as handyman specials with good financing. Instead of complicating the issue any more, I'll leave it at that and let you learn the basics first.

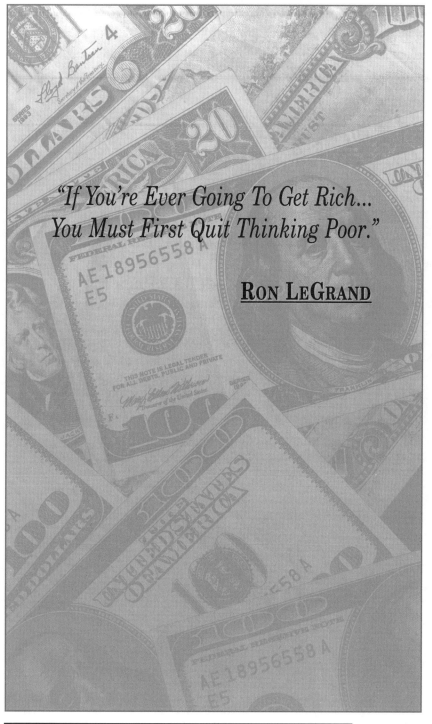

"*If You're Ever Going To Get Rich...*
You Must First Quit Thinking Poor."

RON LeGRAND

*Man's mind, once stretched by a new idea,
never regains its original dimensions.*

Oliver Wendell Holmes

Chapter  16

Profiles
of Success

<u>PHIL BARNES</u>

Phil Barnes was a successful major appliance salesman with one of the most prominent retailers in the country for over 23 years. At 55, he felt he had a secure future: a great job, a good living from his first-rate performance in sales volume, and a reliable plan for retirement. Little did he know, all that was about to change.

Rumors began to float along the corporate grapevine that the company was offering top-level management buyouts and planning a major company-wide re-organization. But employees with Phil's tenure and performance record didn't give them much thought. However, over time, the rumors persisted and intensified. Phil began to feel the need to hedge his bets, to diversify his investment activities. His choice? Real estate.

"I'd never even thought about being involved in real estate. I'd made such good money, the thought never crossed my mind," Phil explains. "But with the rumors of impending change, I felt prompted to give it a try." Phil took what most people thought was the solid way to make money in real estate – he bought a few properties and became a landlord.

"I listened to some tapes from different supposed "gurus" I had heard on television," he recalls. "My perception at the time was that real estate investing was buying a piece of property at 20% down, getting a loan from the bank, putting a tenant in there and hoping you wouldn't have any problems. I believed that's where my income would come from."

But, for Phil, there were problems. "A roof would need replacement, a furnace would blow, and there would go all my profits," Phil recalls. "And I couldn't understand why I wasn't making money! After a few of those, I found out fairly quickly that this was definitely not the way to make money. I had a lot of equity, but I was cash poor. I figured there had to be a better way."

This is when Phil began to look for more information about real estate investing. He became involved in the local Real Estate Investors Association (REIA), a fledgling chapter with only 20 members. "Basically, it was a landlord's gripe group at that time. We were all in the same boat with the same problems. For the most part, the members sat around bemoaning the tax law changes and all the reasons we couldn't get ahead. And nobody wanted to run it, including me. By default, they chose me as president."

Over the next year, Phil's leadership of the local chapter and state chapter involvement paid off in more ways than one. The local chapter's ranks grew to 125 paid members. And through his various activities with the state chapter, he discovered the methods of Ron LeGrand.

"Several of the young investors in the state chapter had heard about some of the hot national-level speakers," Phil recalls. "After investigating several of these speakers, they met Ron. They were so impressed, we arranged for him to come and do a presentation at our state meeting." Phil met Ron at that convention and arranged to have him come speak at an evening meeting of the local chapter. "I was so motivated by what he had to say," Phil explains. "It had that ring of credibility and sincerity that no other real estate investor speaker I had ever heard had."

In the meantime, those rumblings on the corporate grapevine seemed more like prophesy than rumor when company representatives approached Phil and his colleagues with a wage reduction proposal. "It was the beginning of the end as far as I was concerned," Phil states. "They told us that if our earnings were affected negatively by more than 10%, they would offer to buy us out. My salary would have been cut by almost 25%, plus they would have locked in my retirement at that reduced figure, which I thought was ridiculous. So, I decided to take the buy out. It was quite a leap of faith for me."

As a consequence of Ron's earlier visit to the local REIA chapter, Phil arranged to have Ron come back and present a four-day Boot Camp. "The timing was perfect," Phil laughs. "The Boot Camp was scheduled to take place just a couple of months after I took the plunge to be on my own. It couldn't have been better for me."

In addition to great timing, it was a time of great revelation for Phil. "The Boot Camp changed my entire concept of the business," Phil remembers. "Ron taught me how to get my profit up front and forget hoping to get it at the back end. I realized that doing it Ron's way, you can get control of property without ownership, flip it, make your profit, and let somebody else fix the roof!"

This was exactly the kick-start that Phil needed. "Three weeks after Boot Camp, I went back by a For Sale By Owner house we had gotten some information on during the class, but had never talked to anyone about," Phil explains. "I orchestrated a deal with the owner and bought it for $27,000. I put about $5,000 into it to fix it up and sold it for $48,000. So, I made about $18,000 profit on my first deal only three weeks out of Boot Camp. You could say I was very encouraged!"

That deal led to many others. "The worst deal I've ever done still made me money," Phil laughs. "What more can I say than that? Honestly, there have been some deals where I could have made a bit more money, but one of the biggest satisfactions of this work is helping people out. If I can really make a difference and help someone by just sacrificing a little on my end, and still make a nice profit, that means a lot to me. It's one of the reasons I love doing this business."

Phil has taken every Boot Camp offered by Ron. "Ron arms you with all the ammunition you need. And there are so many different aspects to it. I just constantly opened up to different things Ron presented and it's really been good for me. I figured it this way, why re-invent the wheel? Why not take it from somebody who's been there?"

Phil cites several reasons why he thinks Ron's courses are superior to others in the marketplace. "These other guys will tell you you're going to make lots of money, and they give you tons of information. What they don't do is tell you the "how" part of it. What sets Ron LeGrand apart from others is the fact that his information is precise, right to the point, and accurate," he says. "Ron provides a step-by-step system that's understandable and complete. He gives you a lot of information with which you can make money, but just getting the information won't make you any money. Ron provides plenty of follow-up to make sure you know how to take action to implement what you've learned. He's very sincere in wanting you to succeed."

A man with a strong belief in God, Phil is very clear about his values and priorities: God first, family second, then work. "Conservatively speaking, I make at least three times as much money now in half the time as I did working as a salesman," Phil confides. "It would be very easy to get extremely greedy doing this business. I've seen some do that. They just can't believe what they're able to accomplish, and they get obsessed about the amount of money they can make. But I think the key to real fulfillment is balance in all things."

Phil firmly believes that a key to success in this business is taking the time to figure out what others want and need. "This business does not mean that one person profits and the other person has to lose," he explains. "Business is contribution and productivity. It's the process of providing goods and services to people. It's helping people. It's fulfilling needs. If you can figure out what people really want, you'll be rewarded. Show the other guy how he can win, and we both will win."

Another source of satisfaction for Phil is that he is now able to give so much more money and time to others. Recently, Phil took off three weeks, traveled to Haiti and assisted in building a mission church there. "The freedom available by doing this business is wonderful," Phil says. "Now I do whatever things I liko whon I like without having to always worry about fitting in with someone else's schedule, except my wife's, of course."

Phil feels it's never too late for someone to make the transition to this business. "I was into my fifties and I had never seriously considered the notion that I would be anything other than what I was," explains Phil. "I figured I would continue at my job until I retired. My only regret at this point is that I didn't know to do this business sooner."

ELIZABETH BOWERS

Elizabeth Bowers is now in the driver's seat of the car she's dreamed of owning for years – a pearl-white Lexus 400 SL. And she's quick to tell anyone who asks who helped her make her dream come true.

A woman accustomed to working in what, until recently, has been considered primarily a man's domain, Elizabeth had been working as a real estate investor and landlord for 12 years accumulating over 100 rental properties in her Ohio hometown. Then, she explains, something happened that changed her life forever.

"I met Ron LeGrand and listened to him present information on his approach to real estate investing. Suddenly, I realized I had been doing the business all wrong for all those years," Elizabeth recalls. "Ron told me he knew what I was up against. He had a lot of empathy for me. He assured me he was going to help me 'catch up' and show me how to get my business into the '90's.' Since then, my business and my life have gone from what I describe as inefficient to totally efficient. I give Ron a lot of the credit."

Acquiring all her previous real estate knowledge and training from whom she terms "the gurus of the 1980's," Elizabeth spent years in the basements of houses, wearing jeans and overalls and working along side contractors to rehabilitate properties to resell. She laughs heartily when she recalls Ron telling her to get out of the basement.

"Ron taught me how to get out of the dungarees, wear a dress and be professional," she laughs.

Although glad to be out of basements, that working experience has come in very handy. "There's not a contractor alive who can pull one over on me," she explains. "Working in those basements gave me an eagle eye when it comes to estimating repair work, knowing what needs to be done and knowing when it's done correctly."

In addition to pitching in on many "rehab" projects, Elizabeth spent the majority of her time back then as many landlords do – collecting rents, tracking down late payments, fielding complaints and maintaining her properties.

"My property portfolio covered the whole spectrum," she points out. "From the cream of the crop to those in less desirable areas, I had them all."

After attending the Wholesale/Retail Boot Camp in Chicago in 1993, Elizabeth worked diligently over the next year to perfect Ron's craft and became what she terms "very good" at retailing houses. "Ron's information is presented in such a no-nonsense, straightforward way that it's easy to understand, easy to follow and easy to use. Anyone can become good at what he teaches you to do," she explains. When describing the track record of success she experienced just after attending her first Boot Camp, Elizabeth describes it as "surreal...almost spooky." To elaborate she said, "Success happened immediately. It happened so quickly it was magical!"

During this same year, Elizabeth began acting on Ron's advice to trim a significant portion of her rental properties from her portfolio. "And that's exactly what I did," she says. "I took all 100 properties that I owned, analyzed them by property condition and rated them on an 'A to F' grading system. Then, after getting rid of my 'D' and 'F' properties, I re-analyzed all the remaining properties based on mortgage pay-offs. If the property wasn't going to be paid off by the year 2000, I sold it. This left me with only 'A', 'B' or 'C' condition properties which could be paid off before or by the year 2000. This process eliminated all the stress I had experienced owning those lower-quality houses and allowed me to work more efficiently, freeing me up to pursue real estate as a true entrepreneur."

That process, in and of itself, was eye-opening for Elizabeth. What she thought was going to be the foundation of her retirement was really the source of stress and worry. "The 'D' and 'F' grade properties were actually a sieve; a virtual money drain. All the money I was making was going right back out the back door into those rentals. So I had to get rid of those money drains, which were also stealing my energy. Once I got rid of them, I was really in a position to benefit from what Ron had taught me."

Although focused on retailing during the early phase of putting her new-found knowledge into practice, Elizabeth realized that the market in her part of the state was shifting. To remain successful, she realized that she needed to shift her focus. And she did.

"Another great thing about Ron and his courses is that he is an expert in a number of different arenas – retailing, wholesaling, lease/option, for sale by owner, mortgage brokering and others," she points out. "As my market shifted, I could shift with it because, first, I was armed with the information I needed to recognize that it was changing and, secondly, I was equipped to change my focus with it." Now she concentrates on wholesaling lower-end properties to bargain buyers.

Whether retailing or wholesaling, Elizabeth has become very successful at this business by concentrating on deals that consistently make a profit in the $10,000 range. "Repetition is definitely the key to success," she emphasizes. "The printed materials are so well written and so clear, and the information on tape and in the courses so well presented, you just need to focus and do what Ron tells you to do – then do it again and again and again."

When giving advice to others who might be contemplating real estate investment as a business, Elizabeth speaks with conviction, "Attend Ron's Boot Camps! And while you're there, focus!" She also advises to never let your materials get too far out of reach. "Don't ignore the tools that Ron gives you. The written material answers everything. I'm constantly reviewing the information, refreshing my knowledge and learning something new every time I do. It's invaluable!"

Elizabeth points out that her biggest obstacle has been to overcome the tendency to try and re-invent the wheel. "Something in our human nature just urges us to try and improve on something, I'm no exception," she laughs. "But there is no need to do that. And trying to do that just causes problems. He's already been there and done that so you don't have to! If you can just remember that, you're fine!"

Life is very different now for Elizabeth. "I used to wake up and dread every day. Listening to constant complaints from tenants, never-ending maintenance worries on lower-end properties and collecting late rents were all part of what I thought I had to do to be in the real estate business. Since being introduced to Ron's method of real estate, my life has changed. Now, I love my work and I wake up every morning asking myself 'What can I make happen today?'"

Elizabeth is fulfilling all the goals that she ever imagined she could reach through real estate investment – in less than five years she will have no real estate debt, she's making a lot of money, her retirement is already set, and she loves what she does. "I'm solving people's problems and helping them out and that's very fulfilling to me. It makes me happy. I believe happiness is more important than money. And loving what you do is just as important. Now, I have both."

Another reason Elizabeth loves this business is the time it affords her to travel. "I've never been one to yearn for leisure time; however, I do love to travel. I used to travel to try to get away from everything. I would worry the whole time about what was going wrong with those properties. Now, doing the business Ron's way, I travel because I can. And when I go, I actually relax and have fun! I can now honestly say I'm enjoying the journey."

MARK COUSINO

Well into his second successful year as a real estate entrepreneur, Mark Cousino points to three primary things that make this business so fulfilling for him: creating win-win situations, being a master of his own time, and achieving a secure foundation for the future.

Mark had always possessed an entrepreneurial spirit and a desire to obtain an income level and quality of life for himself and his family. He tried his hand in two or three businesses including vending, food concession and computer portraits. "One of the reasons I wanted to work on my own was to be able to take control of my time," explains Mark. "Through my experience I found out that a business can easily take control of you! And there's so much more to life than being obsessed and possessed by your work."

Tired of jobs that controlled his time, earning potential and activities, Mark eventually became "sick and tired of being sick and tired." But that experience can be a very powerful motivating force. He kept searching. Consequently, he found and fell in love with real estate.

"I really didn't know anything about real estate except what I had read in a couple of books," says Mark. "I was sure I could do this on my own through trial and error and the school of hard knocks. I started with a single family home which I bought with bank financing and 25% of my own money. I had no idea at that time about no money down strategies. Even though it was in a rough neighborhood and I got into it heavily with my own cash, I still made a profit from it."

Even though Mark was, as he calls it, "just poking at it with a stick," he could see there was a good deal of potential in real estate. But he felt there must be a way to make the kind of money he wanted without so many headaches and hassles and without so much of his money invested. He began to attend a few Real Estate Investor Association (REIA) meetings and a whole new world opened up.

"I wanted to learn something really different about how this business could work. At REIA, I began to hear of methods of acquiring real estate that eliminated the normal headaches associated with buying, holding, renting and so forth, which is what I had been doing up to that point," explains Mark. "Then I heard of Ron LeGrand at one of these REIA functions. He was offering free subscriptions to his "Quick-Turn" newsletter, so I put my name on the list to receive it."

The information presented by Ron in the newsletter was enough to convince Mark to attend a Real Estate and Entrepreneurs' SuperConference in Orlando, Florida where Ron LeGrand would be a featured speaker. "I heard a number of speakers, each with a specialty. They were experienced, and it was obvious these people had involved themselves directly in the business. They were pros, not just educators," Mark points out. "The conference was a big motivator. To hear some of the newer, cutting edge techniques and strategies that allow you to take control of property without ownership was awesome for me."

After putting quite a bit of money into doing it his own way, Mark was ready to make the necessary adjustments. In December of that year, he proceeded with plans to attend his first Boot Camp. "Ron LeGrand opened my eyes to a whole new world of real estate," says Mark. "I just knew it was going to work. Ron makes it so simple and shows you step-by- step how to produce the results you want. I couldn't compare it to the way I was doing business before."

After the conference, Mark jumped right in. "I got to work right away using the exact ads Ron had shown us in Boot Camp. I created quite a bit of chaos for myself. But I knew I wasn't really going to really learn it until I got in there and did it," he points out. "I got calls immediately. I knew it was going to work. It only took me one deal to know it could be easily duplicated. Ron makes it very simple to follow."

In fact, over the next three months, he had so many success- ful deals, it dawned on him that this business was really taking off. "I didn't have time to do my old business," Mark explains. "It didn't make sense to continue doing something I had been doing for quite some time that wasn't producing the things I really wanted from work."

The timing was just right. Mark made the decision to sell his seasonal business just before the opening of the 1995 season to pursue real estate full-time. "I couldn't go back to what I was doing. The profit I was realizing from doing real estate on a part-time basis was already far exceeding what I could make from my old business," he explains. "Just like Indiana Jones, it was a step of faith."

In addition to SuperConferences, retreats and seminars, Mark has attended both the MLS and Lease Option Boot Camps. He's gained valuable perspective from both, but prefers to spend most of his time orchestrating lease/option deals.

"I prefer working with the homes that need little or no work to be marketable," he points out. "And my favorite aspect is that I provide a service to people who want to own a home, but might not be able to do it the traditional way because of a credit problem. I love the process of educating them, to convince them what everybody else has told them is wrong and that we can get them in a home. It's an unbeatable feeling, and I generate a great monthly cash flow for myself. What could be better?"

"I didn't have a clue as to what I was doing before Ron," Mark says. "And those other guys that are out there in the market who say they can show you how to make money in real estate sure couldn't show me anything that was workable. Ron's 'been there, done that' – really been out there in the trenches doing this business – and he's a great teacher. He's designed a wonderful education for people. But once you've got it, you've got to get out there and do it."

Mark has no sympathy for people who attend Boot Camps and conferences over and over again, but still haven't gotten started with the business. "Ron gives you everything you need to know. If you've studied the courses and gone to the Boot Camp, you're already prepared. What Ron teaches you is enough to go out and flat kill it! You just have to get rid of any 'stinkin' thinkin.' To use a phrase Ron coined, get over your 'analysis paralysis' and do it!"

Mark is able to produce remarkable results from real estate by working 20 to 25 hours a week, leaving plenty of time for those things he enjoys most: his wife and two small children, hunting, fishing, golf, working out and spending time with friends. "Few dads have the opportunity I do. I'm the only dad that gets to take his kid to pre-school and the only one there for T-ball practice and swimming lessons," he points out. "There are more important things than slaving at work. Being a master of my own time is one of the reasons I love this."

Another reason is what he is able to do for his family. "We've always wanted to build our dream house," Mark says. "Profits from this business have allowed us to go ahead and purchase a beautiful 11-acre piece of property for this purpose. Within the next year, construction will be underway. Now I know the kids' college education is taken care of. We're putting money aside for the future, and we definitely don't worry anymore about how next month's bills will be paid!" he adds.

"When I consider some of the things I've accomplished as a result of the information Ron LeGrand has taught me and shared with me, I can't believe it's really happening for me," shares Mark. "It doesn't take a high degree of education. It just takes a willingness to learn. After putting an awful lot of my money into doing it my way, I discovered there was a better way – and Ron's programs showed me how."

RANDY AND CHARLENE FRANCE

When Randy and Charlene were married just a few years ago, they had five children between them, were setting up their new household in a 3-bedroom apartment, and borrowed a car from friends to go on their honeymoon.

"Everything used to be a big deal," Charlene remembers. "Grocery shopping or needing to buy shoes for the kids. If the kids needed shoes, then taking them to Burger King was definitely out."

Have things ever changed for the France family over the last few years!

"We've gone from zero to a six-figure income, from a basement apartment to a $125,000 home being paid off in three years, from borrowing a car in order to have a honeymoon to two brand-new vehicles in the driveway paid off in full," Charlene points out. "We can go anywhere we want. We've traveled more this year than we have in our whole lives. And it's because of the business, because of what we've learned from Ron LeGrand."

The Frances first became involved in real estate by investing in rental properties with a family member. Having heard the concept of quick-turn real estate from various sources, they even tried flipping a couple of houses.

"When we met Ron, we had done a couple of quick-turn deals," explains Charlene. "But we really didn't know what we were doing."

Then a friend invited Randy and Charlene to a Financial Freedom seminar where Ron LeGrand was speaking. "I felt like I was looking at a road map of where we wanted to go," says Charlene. "I couldn't wait to learn more, so I bought the books and tapes right away."

The next step for the Frances was to enroll in an MLS Boot Camp. "It was unbelievable," explains Charlene. "Before the Boot Camp, it was if we were trying to put together a complicated machine or toy with no instructions and we always had pieces left over. You spend a couple of days with Ron and he puts all the missing pieces together. All of a sudden everything fit together. Here was a guy that was doing exactly what I wanted to do and doing it the right way and making money."

"By the time we left the seminar, we knew what to do, we knew how to do it, we knew how to look for them and how to repair them," Randy adds. "The information Ron gave us is complete information. Ron is not 'just a suit', he's one of us. He knows this business so well because he does it himself. He's not dressed up in a $2,000 suit worried about how his hair looks the whole time. He spoon feeds the information to you, but he never looks down his nose at you. He's just an everyday guy that people can relate to."

Immediately following the Boot Camp in Chicago, Charlene had to have emergency gall bladder surgery. She was about to find out just how easy the business can be. Still recuperating in the hospital, she bought and resold her first wholesale house lying on her back. "I made $6,000 from my hospital bed," Charlene laughs. "I bought the house for $15,000 and sold it six days later for $21,000. So we made $1,000 a day! It gave me an attitude of 'My God, I can do this!'"

Prior to progressing from part-time to full time in real estate,

Charlene worked in human resources for a retail store making about $15,000 a year. When one of her first deals brought in about $22,000 profit for the Frances, it was definitely a break-through. "It was then that I realized I couldn't afford to work for anybody else," she explains. "It was time for me to go for it!"

"You know, I love this business," she chirps. "It's so much fun! When you find a house, there's so much you can do with it. You can flip it, you can re-hab it and put a family into it, you can keep it, you can lease option it," explains Charlene. "Ron teaches you how to be a real estate entrepreneur, not a real estate investor. He teaches you how to control a property and orchestrate deals. Often, the seller and the new buyer are at the closing table with us or within a few hours and we walk away with cash profits right then and there. Other times, we may take title, hold the property for as little as a few days to a few weeks, then 'turn it' and get instant cash profits."

Charlene is a great believer in attending Ron's conferences over and over again. "You never get done learning," she advises. "And we can make thousands from just one new idea Ron gives us. For instance, Randy and I had been showing homes to almost all interested callers and wasting a lot of our time. Ron advised us to run credit reports prior to showing the home. Now we don't show a home unless it's to a qualified buyer. That one idea has saved us tens of thousands of dollars."

The Frances are maintaining approximately 35 to 40 lease/option properties while they buy and renovate other properties. "Every time we sell a house we pick up another lease/option so we can keep our monthly income coming in while we're rehabbing and selling homes," explains Charlene.

The Frances enjoy the aspect of creating liveable houses. "I could never understand all these houses that looked horrible and were just sitting there vacant.. Now we buy junkers, go in and gut them, re-do them and make them a home for somebody. It's such a rush for me!"

Ninety percent of the homes they re-hab and sell are sold to single mothers. "Having been a single mom with three kids myself, I can remember plenty of tearful times when all I could afford to feed my children was crackers. I know what kind of obstacles these women are up against. It's the greatest feeling in the world to be able to help these women get into homes of their own."

"Once we bought a house that was condemned and the city was going to tear it down," Charlene continues. "We actually had to get a court order to keep them from demolishing it. We were able to buy this house for $5,000. We fixed it up and sold it. Now, instead of that being an empty lot, it's a home, a family a single mom and her three kids live there. No one would give her a chance. Now those kids are going to remember having Christmas in that living room. And we made a very decent profit on it, too. It doesn't get much better than that!"

Their involvement in real estate has completely changed the lives of the Frances and their children in every way, but one - their values remain totally intact. "We could make a lot more money than we do," Charlene says. "But there's so much more to this for us than just making the money. It's giving a single mom and her kids the chance to move into a decent house in a decent neighborhood. It's about showing other people they can do this, too. It's about giving back what you receive."

Another way the Frances give to others is by supporting them in learning the business. "Once a month we hold meetings to introduce people to real estate entrepreneuring," says Charlene. "One young woman we've been mentoring has a husband who has, until recently, been totally opposed to her involvement in real estate. Once she bought her brand-new 24-foot pleasure boat, he finally realized there might be something of value to this!" The boat's name? "Rent-to-Own!"

"I can't think of how life could get any better for us," Charlene says. "Our home is paid, our cars are paid, college for our kids is already set. This business is the neatest opportunity. Our lives have changed so much! It's given us such freedom. Everything used to be such a big deal – even buying groceries. Now paying for a year of college is one deal! And I get such pleasure from blessing other people. Even though this was years ago when we were just getting started, I'll never forget what a joy it was to be able to go and buy new carpet for my mother. She had always helped me so much, it was such a joy to help her. And I was able to pay for the whole thing with a check!"

Another big blessing in the Frances' lives is the ability to travel with their family. "We've traveled more in the last two years than we've traveled in our whole lives," Charlene explains. "We've taken two cruises just in the last six months! And none of us will ever forget the Christmas we leased an ocean front condo in Cocoa Beach and spent two weeks at having the time of our lives as a family! The kids were thrilled, especially spending Christmas at Disney World!"

When advising her apprentices, Charlene tells them, "Go to Ron's conferences and seminars and listen, listen, listen! The business can take you wherever you want to go. But don't get greedy; don't do it just for the money. Stay around people that are doing the business, and don't forget where you came from!" Sounds like sound advice.

RICHARD KANSA

Richard Kansa recently fulfilled a long-standing dream – to underwrite a trip for his mother and aunt so they could return to their homeland of Austria-Hungary. Now in her 70's, Richard's mother had not seen the place where she was born since immigrating (in the early 1940's) at the start of World War II. She'd not seen her cousins since they were all small children. She'd never visited the spot where her grandparents, who had been alive when she left, were buried.

"I had made up a dream list when I first entered the real estate business as a full-time entrepreneur," explains Richard. "I remember telling myself if I didn't identify the things I really wanted to do and start doing them, it simply wasn't going to happen. Accompanying my mother and her sister back to Vienna, treating them to a reunion with the family still in Europe, and being there with them to savor the experience was at the top of my list."

Words escape Richard when he tries to describe witnessing the reunion scene on the train platform in Vienna. "It was worth the whole trip," he says. "I just can't tell you what it was like for these people to see one another again for the first time in over 50 years. So much emotion, so many tears. Squeals and screams of recognition filled the train platform. They met family they never even knew they had. At her first opportunity after we left the train station, my mom bent down to touch the ground. She was home again."

Richard wants the person who made it possible for the trip to take place to know that he played an important role in making his mom's dream come true.

"Ron LeGrand not only taught me this business, he took a personal interest in my success. Right in the beginning, he gave me his home phone number and encouraged me to call him if I needed help. I found that I did indeed need some help in the beginning and I thought if he was dumb enough to give me his number, I'm going to be brave enough to call him."

The personal support Richard received from Ron helped him over his first hump and two weeks later he had his first house under contract. He flipped it and made his first profit as a real estate entrepreneur – $5,000!

"Ron teaches how to make money in real estate, but he also points out so many things that make such a positive difference in your life," Richard says. "For instance, how valuable time is, how important it is for you to leverage your time in order to do the things you want to do, and that someday is now! If Ron wasn't doing what he does, I wouldn't be doing what I do. And doing what I do gave me the time and money to make my mom's dream come true. Talk about job perks!"

Richard was working as an employee trainer and counselor for various client companies all over the U.S. when he first began to give real estate some thought as an investment opportunity. "A colleague of mine suggested we go to a real estate seminar given by some outfit out of Orlando," Richard explains. "I, along with many other attendees, didn't understand anything that they talked about and found it not at all useful. I left with the feeling that I wasted four days of my life."

Despite that disappointing experience, Richard persisted in his quest to find some usable and credible information about real estate investing. He called the president of the local chapter of the Real Estate Investors Association. "I figured if anyone could tell me anything worth knowing, it would be him. He told me Ron LeGrand was the best in the business and that copies of his book would be available at their next meeting," recalls Richard. "I came to the next meeting, got my copy of the book, and basically read almost half of it while the speaker was doing his presentation. I was fascinated."

Skeptical since being burned by his first experience, Richard called Ron's office and talked to Ray Rach. "I asked Ray if this stuff really worked and if it would work in my area of the country," Richard explains. "He called and set up conference calls with students from all over the country to talk to me about their successes. I signed up for a Boot Camp right then and there." Thinking Ray had told him the conference would be held in Nashville, Richard made plane reservations to get to the event.

"I called Ray back to ask him what there was to do in Nashville and he asked me why would I be interested in Nashville night life. He informed me that the Boot Camp was being held in Asheville, not Nashville," Richard laughs. "I had to ask Ray where the hell is Asheville? We still laugh about that one!"

However, he did get his reservations straight and made it to Asheville to attend the Boot Camp. It's a good thing he did. "I knew right away, I'd say within an hour, that this was exactly the information I wanted," says Richard. "I knew immediately that it was what I was going to do even though I was about as ignorant as anyone could be in the field. I had never met a REALTOR® and didn't even know what a title company did."

After leaving the Boot Camp, Richard summarized all the segments of real estate he didn't fully understand and made a list. He set a goal for himself to knock one item off the list each week. "I decided that I would learn something every week," explains Richard. "One week I called a couple of different title companies and asked them to explain to me what it was they did. Most were happy to help." Richard was still working full-time at this point and delving into real estate on a part-time basis. "It was like having two full-time jobs," he points out. "But I told myself that if I could make enough money to live on in six months, I would do this business full-time."

By the end of the six-month period, Richard had purchased three houses, flipped two and had one under contract. He had made $5,000 on his first flip, $3,500 profit on a second flip and $17,000 on his first retail deal. "I thought that was pretty good for my first deals," he adds. "You know a lot of people were telling me a lot of negative stuff during that period, but I just drew on what Ron had told us. Don't listen to negative people and just apply what you learned. He's right. According to Richard, there isn't any niche of this business that hasn't made him money. "It's been a big learning experience and a period of growth. Sure, I've made some mistakes, but that's part of it. I've made a profit on everything I've done. It's been incredible. I'm now moving away from re-habbing and moving more aggressively into owner-financing. I've got some very interesting things happening now in that arena."

"I love this work," Richard continues. "Working at a job was something I found very confining. It goes back to a personality thing. Work should be an extension of who you are. When someone asks me how many hours a week I work at this, I honestly can't say. It's so much a part of who I am. Only when I worked at a regular job did I know how many hours I worked. To me, what I'm doing now is not work. It's a perfect fit for me."

Describing the tangible and intangible changes that have taken place in his life, Richard says, "What life is about now is the difference between just existing and really knowing what it's like to be alive. This business is a progressive business – one where you can certainly get rich, there's no doubt about that. But you know, rich is a relative term. How much is enough? Being able to do what I want to do when I want to do it and having the means to do it makes me a very lucky man."

STEVE POWANDA

While attending the University of Pittsburgh to obtain a degree in information science, Steve Powanda spent a significant amount of time reading and studying books and tapes focused on a totally different subject: how to be your own boss. It wouldn't be until years later that he would realize his dream.

Having acquired his four-year degree, Steve set off to join the corporate world as a software designer and computer programmer at a Washington, D.C. area company. Then, back in Pittsburgh, he spent the next six years with a financial services company. Still intrigued and pursuing entrepreneurial information, Steve began to come across books on real estate and to read about those who were good at creating wealth from investing in real estate. He hungered to know more.

Steve began his real estate career by purchasing a few rental properties. Although he describes the deals as "not bad," the enterprise didn't turn out as well as he had hoped. "For the amount of money, time and effort I spent, I sure didn't see the return I wanted," explains Steve. "As a result, I found myself becoming very disillusioned with it."

It was then he joined an American Congress of Real Estate (ACRE) group whose membership consisted primarily of people buying and fixing property and then renting to tenants. "I was hoping to meet people who were doing what I was interested in doing," Steve recalls. "My experience was very limited, but I knew there was a another way to make a living from real estate other than the way I had been doing it."

Just about that time, the ACRE group had a speaker give a presentation on his method of "quick-turning" real estate. "Despite all my reading and searching, I had never heard anything quite like this before," says Steve. "He got my attention with his 'buy and sell' wisdom versus the conventional 'buy and hold' rhetoric offered up by most other so-called experts. I bought a paperback book Ron was offering at his presentation. I began reading it immediately. It was extremely interesting." In fact, the content of that little book fascinated Steve and prompted him to attend the next scheduled SuperConference where Ron would be speaking. "I could tell by reading his book that this guy was the real thing," Steve comments. "I knew he must be a real estate entrepreneur on a very serious level, not just a guy out there making a living on the seminar circuit."

At the SuperConference, Steve was able to hear and meet a number of people doing extremely well in this business, many on a large scale. "I was now considering doing this eventually on a full-time basis," explains Steve. "I was definitely not interested in any rinky-dink, part-time business opportunity. This SuperConference showed me that Ron LeGrand was offering a system that was valid, something I could master and turn into a legitimate and successful full-time business. It was just what I wanted."

By the end of the SuperConference, Steve made a decision to proceed to the next level by registering for a Boot Camp. "The information presented in the Boot Camp was totally different than anything I had ever heard of," recalls Steve. "It opened up so many doors of possibility for me. And one great thing happened there. I drew first option on a property our group negotiated on during our 'hands-on' bus trip. I took the option. That really helped me because it forced me to do something immediately following the conference."

At the same time he was working on that deal, he began hunting down some deals of his own. He also started setting up goals for himself. "I don't think of goals necessarily as dollar amounts," Steve points out. "That can sometimes work against you. Instead I shoot for the number of deals I want to do, and look to increase it year after year." Steve's initial goals would act as guideposts for him during that first year.

Unfortunately, he actually lost a couple of hundred dollars on the house he inherited from Boot Camp. Steven looks back at it as his chance to get all his mistakes out of the way early on in his career. "I always say, if you're going to make mistakes, make them in the beginning and lose $500 as opposed to making them later on and losing $5,000," laughs Steve. "I play the stock market. Losses are part of the game. You just try to make them as small as possible. Of course, there are a lot of people in this business who make profits right from the very first deal. I just didn't happen to be one of them."

"Actually, in this business your proficiency becomes more keen as you go along," he continues. "I always tell people the more you do the better you get. Your ability increases and your learning continues. The important thing is to get that first one done and over with!"

His next deal was an true inspiration. "The next deal I did

was a fixer-upper I bought, renovated and sold," Steve reports. "I bought it for about $17,000 and sold it for approximately $48,000. I ended up making about $18,000 net profit on it. Just goes to show, you win some, you lose some! Except for that first deal, I've made money on everything I've done." By the end of his first year, Steven had scratched off every item he had placed on his original goal sheet. He was earning almost twice as much in real estate as he did from his regular job. It was decision time. He knew there were new targets to aim for.

Steve announced his plans to his employers and his family. Although it was difficult leaving what Steve considered a good job, an above-average salary, great benefits, a prestigious company and what most people in Pittsburgh view as the ultimate in security, he had reached his decision.

His family thought he was crazy. His friends worried. Trusted colleagues just shook their heads. "It was the hardest thing I'd ever done in my life," admits Steve. "But I had come to the point where I could no longer work what were essentially two full-time jobs at the same time. I was, as they say, at the point of no return. It was time to chart my own destiny; to make as much money as I felt I was worth; to be my own boss," Steve says. "I had diligently sought this opportunity, and the time was now!"

He has no regrets. "Looking back, I only wish I had been more aggressive at the outset," Steve says. I was really extra cautious. Instead of getting one deal complete before beginning to locate the next one, I would have sought them out and stacked them up in the pipeline. There's a lot to be said for going out there and getting four or five things moving at the same time."

Involved in wholesale, retail and a small amount of owner financing, Steve's favorite niche is retail: locating the distressed properties, fixing them up and re-selling them. "Typically, people are willing to let the distressed properties go for a lot less money and this can create good profit margins," advises Steve. "And just like Ron teaches, if you have the ability to look past how ugly it is to its true value and profit potential, you can force the market value up and do really well for yourself."

One of Steve's best deals was a wholesale deal. "It was so

easy," recalls Steve. "From the time I bought it to the day I sold it, everything just fell into place. I sold it three days after I bought it and made a $12,000 profit without ever even touching it! Of course, they don't come along like that every day, but it's a big thrill when it happens every now and then."

Steve's current goals include upping the number of properties he buys during the next year to 50 or 60 and focusing more on owner financing. "I originally thought you needed money to make money, but as I go along I'm finding that when you find good deals, the money will come," he continues. "I mean there are a lot of people who have a lot of money and are more than happy to lend it to you if the deal is good. And one of the things I learned from Ron is how to tell what is a good deal versus a bad one. It's been incredibly valuable knowledge."

Steve attends Ron's live events again and again. "I learn something every time I go," explains Steve. "And Ron teaches exactly what he does himself. I've gone down to Jacksonville and seen where he does his work. He does this on a day-to-day basis. So he's constantly gaining insights and better ways all the time that he continually shares with his students."

Life has changed quite a bit for Steve since becoming an entrepreneur. "Besides leaving my job and waving good-bye to corporate life, it's enjoying the freedom to organize my life the way I want it," says Steve. "It's a business and I manage myself accordingly. But I love being able to take several get away vacations during the year. I take a lot of mini-vacations throughout the year. I just came back from a week at Greenleaf Resort near Orlando where I was playing golf, tennis and just hanging out because it's such a nice place. I enjoy being able to do that."

At twenty-nine years of age, Steven finds himself working at a career he loves, reaping rewards he feels confident will only continue to increase. Completely debt-free, he prefers to pay cash for everything, including new automobiles and those vacations. "Most everybody I know lives with major debt on everything they own," explains Steve. "I'm so thankful I don't have to do that."

*Losers labor under the impression
that winners never fail.*

Anonymous

Chapter

Succeeding While Others Fail

The number-one cause of failure in this business is not trying. The second is ignorance. Just the fact you have bought this book sets you apart from the crowd. I have negotiated with hundreds of real estate owners who have never bought a single book on the subject. You are different. Armed with what you have learned here, you have every reason to succeed in real estate investment. Nothing in this book, however, will do the work for you; you must get out and try. And while you're out there taking action, continue to learn as much as you can from every source possible.

Everybody hits stumbling blocks. Remember, you are not alone in this. Later in this chapter, I have included a list of every possible cause of failure in this business and the way to respond to each. The list will help you pinpoint a problem and then work to correct it. If, for any reason, it seems you're spinning your wheels and getting nowhere, just read this chapter again. The cause of your problem and its solution are mentioned somewhere.

The only failure that counts, because it can stop you cold, is mistakenly believing that winners never fail. Remember, only losers use failure as an excuse for giving up. Winners expect to overcome and learn from their failures. They realize they are problem solvers and believe they will always win somehow. If you think about it, I'll bet you agree that even the bad things that have happened in your life have had a good effect on your future.

POSSIBLE PROBLEMS

The list of causes of failure is self-explanatory, but it would be useful to highlight some of the key points.

Fear heads the list because of its unique power to paralyze an investor. So many people fear making offers. Why? Fear of rejection. What is the worst thing that can happen to you if you make an offer? Have you ever heard of someone's getting hurt while making an offer? Some owners may get mad if you make a ridiculous, low-ball offer, but so what? Some will accept the offer, and thank you later for it!

Are you afraid of being chased off the seller's property? Unlikely! Especially if you tell people over the phone, even before you go to the house, how you do business. Remind them there is nothing personal about the offer; it's just numbers. If it works for them, great. If it doesn't, you'll buy another house. If you're still scared to make those offers, hire someone else to make them for you. You can promise your negotiator part of the profit you make when you close, or just pay him a flat fee.

Better yet, hire a buyer's broker to work for you. They usually get paid at the closing from the seller's proceeds, thus there's no cost to you. A buyer's broker is simply an agent who declares he or she represents the buyer in the transaction. They are becoming active in most areas of the country and could be a valuable asset if you are afraid to make offers or simply don't have the time or knowledge to do so. You can find buyer's brokers by simply asking agents if they act in that capacity. If they don't, they should be able to refer you to the right people.

I use a simple philosophy that helps keep me on track and helps overcome some of the negative responses from REALTORS® and sellers — **SW SW SW SW**: *Some Will, Some Won't, So What, Someone's Waiting*!

Everybody makes mistakes. Just don't use them to make excuses. So what if you make a mistake? Every successful real estate investor you will ever meet has made more mistakes than you! That's how they know more than you. Just get on with it and accept mistakes as the necessary cost of being alive and in business.

You're going to make mistakes and you know it. Start making them now so you can correct them and make some more. Another word for mistake is experience. Few wealthy people lack experience.

Fear of financial loss is another big fear. If this is your fear, then only make deals that don't require your own money and protect yourself from all personal liability. No one should feel he or she has to risk vast sums of life savings to succeed in real estate!

You never have to borrow money from a bank. You don't need cash or credit to invest in real estate. Even in the case of a buy low-sell high retail-type deal, which is the only one that might require money, the money can be put up by investors attracted to good deals. Be conservative if you like; work with sandwich lease options, and use no money at all! However, understand that until you overcome that fear of financial loss, you will be missing out on some of the fun and profit. Keep your risks small so you can keep your losses small. If you lose one now and then, so what! Make it up on the next one.

FEARING THE UNKNOWN

Fear of the unknown and of how to structure a deal require just one solution: Get help! It seems the more knowledgeable an investor, the more likely they are to call in an expert when they are in unfamiliar territory. Asking for help when you need it is a sign you are on the right track. See to it you get enough education to start moving. You don't have to know everything to start. You will learn as you go. Just get enough information to start, and call in help as you need it. Use competent professionals and experienced investors as your mentors.

The last thing you should do is get help from someone who knows less than you do. Everyone has an opinion. Value only those opinions that come from people who have "walked the walk," not just "talked the talk." Bad advice can cost you much more than no advice.

Procrastination is the big killer. It kills deals, profits and enthusiasm. Make offers, even if just to keep up the momentum of your business. On a part-time basis, you should make four or five offers each week. On a full-time basis, you should make 20 or 30 offers a week. Remember, you don't have to type up a contract to make an offer. Just sketch it out on a piece of paper so the seller gets the idea. If he says yes, then write it up. By using REALTORS®, you literally can submit several offers at once, thus leveraging your time.

Don't try to go it alone. Some people can, but many successful investors work better with partners. It's more fun with partners, especially spouses. You can bounce ideas off them and see their reaction. And this is one business where you can convert a good idea into hard cash in a matter of days. However, it's also important, from the standpoint of motivation, to surround yourself with positive-thinking people. You can form mastermind groups in areas of common interest. This is a powerful resource, particularly when the group is made up of individuals who are working the same business, trying to accomplish the same goals.

I remember when I was a novice investor. All I wanted to talk about was real estate. Consequently, I only hung around with other real estate-minded people. When I met people who wanted to talk about something else, we had a short conversation. I couldn't wait to get started in the morning. I looked forward to every day with a passion.

The message is: **DO SOMETHING YOU LOVE!**

I warn you, though, stay away from negative thinkers and deadheads. It is especially important, as a beginning investor, to avoid taking advice from those who have not succeeded. Have you ever noticed that everyone has an opinion about real estate? Even people who have never owned a piece of property give advice! I recommend you listen only to real investors who are making more than you. When looking for mentors, surround yourself with people who have demonstrated that they possess knowledge and experience.

A mastermind group is a powerful insurance program for success. I received a letter from Joe Bowman in Ft. Lauderdale about the results of just such a group — one that was formed from our Boot Camp there in February 1992.

Joe's letter said this group of six had made 125 offers in the month after I left. They had bought 25 houses, and several hot offers were still pending. This wasn't done as a partnership or a group effort. It was the sum of their individual offers. He tells me it's much easier to talk with people who have the same training and have the same objectives. Besides, it's so much more fun to celebrate your successes when you get friends involved.

By the way, I didn't hear the profit figures on those 25 houses, but I'd be willing to bet, if my students bought them, there is at least $300,000 to $500,000 net profit involved.

MORE PRACTICAL TIPS

Don't try to make repairs yourself. Hire someone to do them. Ask yourself, "Do I want to be paid as a painter or as an investor?" If you repair the houses yourself, you may become discouraged in this business. Your time would be better put to use making offers. One deal that generates $10,000 profit will pay for a lot of labor!

You need to take control of your own life. Good management can free up a lot of your time so you can accomplish more and enjoy life to the hilt. Manage your time; don't let your time manage you. Plan your activities using a daily planner. Chart your course before you start. Know your goals and your destination. Plan how to get there, and take action.

Stay focused and do not allow yourself to get sidetracked. Remember to work in a little time every day to learn something new. Knowledge ultimately saves time as well as money.

Remember the spaghetti theory, and how it applies to making lots of offers. If you throw enough spaghetti against the wall, some of it is bound to stick! Similarly, if you make a sufficient number of good offers, meaning, of course, offers profitable for you yet tailored to the needs of the seller, you can count on some of them being accepted. It matters little if many people say no when all you need is an occasional yes. That one yes can make you more money than some people make in an entire year.

Chasing too many dead leads is a problem that cures itself quickly. Most investors only need a little practice to realize the value of carefully screening prospects over the telephone. High gasoline bills and lack of time teach very quickly the value of checking out your leads with key questions before committing your time and money.

Life has few certainties, but the greatest hazard in life is to risk nothing. A popular saying among real estate investors is, "If you will do what others won't for five years, you can do what others can't for the rest of your life."

Throughout this book, I have mentioned just a few of my successful students and their stories. I truly wish I could write about them all, but frankly, there are just too many to give all of them the credit they deserve in the space available.

You know who you are, and I hope you understand why your name wasn't mentioned. I'd have to write a book the size of the Los Angeles phone book to include all of you. I truly appreciate your letters and faxes about your successes. It's what makes us tick around my office, and I hope they never stop coming in. Take time to write down your success story and send it to us with your photo. You'll enjoy the process and at the same time brighten our day. Besides, you never know when we'll make you famous like the folks in this book.

I want all of you to be the best you can be, and I hope all your parents have rich children.

SUCCESS TIPS

- Take care of your cash-flow needs first, before you try to build wealth. Keep working until your real estate cash flow is equal to or exceeds your income from a job. Then you don't have to worry about making a living. You can start making money.

- Stay focused! Stay on track! Stick to your game plan! If it works, don't even think of anything else, just keep doing it. Don't stray and, above all, keep heading for your goal.

- Take advice only from someone who is making more money than you. Learn from people who are doing. Don't be afraid to ask for help. The experts all use expert advice. It saves money.

- Make your profit going in. Profit is not borrowed money. Borrowed money has to be paid back. Negotiate good deals and don't depend on appreciation.

- Movement is the key. You have to get out and do things. You will make mistakes, but don't let them stop you. You have to keep it moving. Start somewhere. You may not get rich quick, but if you don't start, you'll never get rich.

- Avoid listening to negative thinkers and deadheads. They are everywhere. The people who are closest to you are usually the most negative. Many people will never understand what you're doing, if you're doing it right. Leave them in your dust; don't let them bury you in their dirt.

- Deal only with motivated sellers. I probably said this a dozen times in this book. But if you ever catch yourself wasting time with a seller, and feeling generally discouraged in looking for deals, the root of the problem is almost always a lack of seller motivation. You don't want to chase dead-end leads. So screen the sellers well over the phone before you drive anywhere.

- Make a lot of offers. Don't get bogged down in doing the wrong things. Concentrate on activities that produce the most income. Nothing produces more than making offers. If you don't make offers, you won't make deals.

- Make a reservation to attend the very next Boot Camp you can. This valuable hands-on training cannot be found anywhere else. It will save you thousands of dollars in mistakes and give you a focused, easy-to-follow plan to generate cash. You simply cannot afford the mistakes that come with trial and error when such an inexpensive Quick-Start opportunity is available. **Take action now. You'll be glad you did.**

- Call or write my office for more information on our full line of training material and events. See page 280 for details.

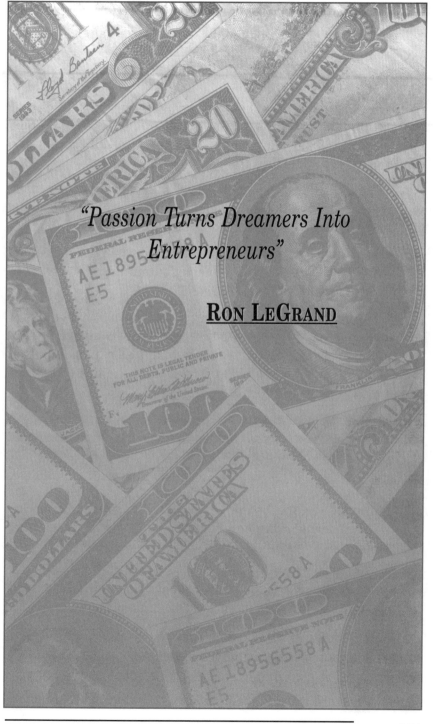

"Passion Turns Dreamers Into Entrepreneurs"

RON LeGRAND

GLOSSARY OF
REAL ESTATE TERMS

Affidavit: A written statement or declaration sworn to or affirmed before an authorized person.

Agreement of Sale: A written agreement in which the purchaser agrees to buy and the seller agrees to sell. Terms and conditions are included in the agreement.

Alienation Clause: Also known as a "due-on-sale" clause. This is a provision that allows a lender to demand payment of the balance of a loan in full if the collateral is sold.

Amortization Mortgage: A debt for which the periodic repayments are used to reduce the principal outstanding as well as to pay off the current interest charges.

Apportionment: The adjustment of the income, expenses, or carrying charges of real estate that is usually computed to the date of closing of title so that the seller pays all expenses to that date. The buyer assumes all expenses from the date on which the deed is conveyed to the buyer.

Appraisal: An estimate of a property's value made by an appraiser who is usually presumed to be an expert in this work.

Appraisal by Comparison: An estimate of value made by comparing the sale prices of other similar properties.

Assignment: The method or manner by which a right or contract is transferred from one person (the assignor) to another (the assignee).

Assumption of Mortgage: This occurs when a person takes title to property and assumes the payment of an existing note or deed of trust.

Balloon Payment: A final installment payment, larger than previous installments, that pays off a debt.

Beneficiary: The person who receives or is to receive the benefits of a certain act.

Bird Dog/Bird Dogger: A person who looks for houses that potentially fit the guidelines of the properties that you prefer to purchase. Bird doggers will bring the information that you require and you will reimburse them for their efforts on whatever basis you have agreed upon.

Bona Fide: In good faith; without fraud.

Capital Gain or Loss: The difference between the basis price (cost plus purchase expenses) of a capital asset and its sales price.

Caveat Emptor: Let the buyer beware. The buyer must examine the goods or property and buy at his or her own risk.

Chain of Title: A history of the conveyances and encumbrances affecting a title from the time the original patent was granted or as far back as records are available.

Client: The principal: the one who employs a broker and who compensates a broker.

Closing Date: The date on which the buyer takes over the property.

Cloud on the Title: An outstanding claim or encumbrance that, if valid, would affect or impair the owner's title.

Codicil: An addition to or amendment of a will.

Collateral: Additional security pledged for the payment of a debt.

Commission: A fee charged for brokerage services.

Commitment: A pledge; a promise; an affirmation agreement.

Complaint: 1. In civil law, the initial statement of the facts on which a complaint is based. 2. In criminal law, the preliminary charge made against the accused.

Comps: See Appraisal by Comparison.

Condemnation: The acquisition of private property for public use with fair compensation to the owner. See also Eminent Domain.

Conditional Sales Contract: A contract for the sale of property stating that although delivery is to be made to the buyer, the title is to remain vested in the seller until the conditions of the contract have been fulfilled.

Consideration: Anything given as an inducement to enter into a contract, such as money or personal services. Any contract, lease, obligation, or mortgage may subsequently be modified without consideration provided that the change is made in writing and signed.

Contract: A legally enforceable agreement.

Covenants: Agreements written into deeds and other instruments promising performance or non-performance of certain acts or stipulating certain uses or restrictions on the property.

Debt Service: Annual amount to be paid by a debtor for money borrowed.

Deed: An instrument in writing, duly executed and delivered, that conveys title to real property.

Deed Restriction: A restriction imposed in a deed to limit the use of the land. A deed might include clauses preventing the sale of liquor or defining the size, type, value, or placement of improvements.

Default: Failure to fulfill a duty or promise or to discharge an obligation; omission or failure to perform an act. In property foreclosure, usually the failure to pay loan installment repayments when they become due.

Defeasance Clause: The clause in a mortgage that permits the mortgagor to redeem his or her property upon payment of the obligations to the mortgagee.

Defendant: The party sued or called to answer in any lawsuit, civil or criminal.

Deficiency Judgment: When the security for a loan is sold for less than the amount of the loan, the unpaid amount (the deficiency) is held by law (the judgment) to be the liability of the borrower unless the new owner has assumed the debt.

Due-on-Sale: See Alienation Clause.

Earnest Money: Down payment made by a purchaser of real estate as evidence of good faith.

Easement: A right that may be exercised by the public or individuals on, over, or through the property of others.

Eminent Domain: A right of the government to acquire property for public use. The owner must be fairly compensated.

Encroachment: A building, part of a building, or obstruction that intrudes on the property of another.

Encumbrance: Any right to or interest in property interfering with its use or transfer or subjecting it to an obligation. In connection with foreclosure property, the most likely encumbrances are mortgages and claims for unpaid taxes.

Equity: In real estate, the difference between the value of a property and the amount owed on it. Also called the owner's interest.

Equity Loan: Junior (subordinate) loan based on a percentage of the equity.

Escrow: A written agreement between two or more parties providing that certain instruments or property be entrusted to a third party to be delivered to a designated person upon the fulfillment or performance of some act or condition.

Estate: The degree, quantity, nature and extent of interest (ownership) that a person has in real property.

Estoppel Certificate: An instrument executed by the mortgagor setting forth the status of and the balance due on the mortgage as of the date of the execution of the certificate.

Eviction: A legal proceeding by a landlord to recover possession of real property.

Exclusive Agency: An agreement to employ one broker only. If the sale is made by any other broker, both are entitled to commissions.

Exclusive Right to Sell: An agreement to give a broker the exclusive right to sell for a specified period. If a sale during the term of the agreement is made by the owner or by any other broker, the broker holding the exclusive right is, nevertheless, entitled to compensation.

Executor: A person or a corporate entity or any other type of organization named in a will to carry out its provisions.

Fee (fee simple, fee absolute): The absolute ownership of real property. This type of estate gives the owner and his or her heirs unconditional power of disposition.

FHA: Federal Housing Administration. See FHA Mortgage Loan.

FHA Mortgage Loan: Mortgage loan insured by the Federal Housing Administration.

Fiduciary: A person who transacts business or handles money or property on behalf of another. The relationship implies great confidence and trust.

First Mortgage: Mortgage that has priority as a lien over all other mortgages. In cases of foreclosure, the first mortgage will be satisfied before other mortgages are paid off.

Foreclosure: A procedure whereby property pledged as security for a debt is sold to pay the debt in the event of default in payments or terms.

Grace Period: Additional time allowed to perform an act or make a payment before a default occurs.

Grantee: The party to whom the title to real property is conveyed; the buyer

Grantor: The person who conveys real estate by deed; the seller.

Habendum Clause: The "to have and to hold" clause that defines or limits the quantity of the estate granted in the deed.

HUD: Department of Housing and Urban Development. This agency has a broad mission in the entire housing industry. The specific area of interest to you, as an investor, is its involvement in subsidizing rents for low-income housing and the marketing of repossessed houses. Many of the HUD repos provide EXCELLENT investment opportunities.

Hypothecate: To use something as security without giving up possession of it.

Installments: Parts of the same debt, payable at successive periods as agreed; payments made to reduce a mortgage.

Intestate: A person who dies before making a will, or whose will is defective in form.

Irrevocable: Incapable of being recalled or revoked; unchangeable; unalterable.

Joint Tenancy: Ownership of property by two or more persons, each of whom has an undivided interest with or without the right of survivorship.

Judgment: Decree of a court declaring that one individual is indebted to another, and fixing the amount of such indebtedness.

Junior Mortgage: A mortgage second in lien (subordinate) to a previous mortgage.

Landlord: One who rents property to another.

Land Contract: In reality, a land contract is a promise to pay. In other words, if you buy a house under a land contract, you promise to pay an agreed-upon amount on or before a specific date. Once the terms have been fulfilled, the seller will then deed the property to you.

Land Trust: A means of taking control of a property anonymously. The only name that will appear on public records will be the name of the trust and, usually, the name of the trustee. The land trust provides some asset protection in that it requires a good deal of digging via legal channels to discover if a person is the beneficiary of a trust.

Lease: A contract whereby, for a consideration, usually termed rent, one who is entitled to the possession of real property transfers such rights to another for life, for a term of years, or at will.

Leasehold: The interest given to a lessee of real estate by a lease.

Lessee: A person to whom property is rented under a lease.

Lessor: One who rents property to another under a lease.

Lien: A legal right or claim on a specific property that attaches to the property until a debt is satisfied.

Life Estate: The conveyance of title to property for the duration of the life of the grantee.

Lis Pendens: A legal document filed in the office of the county clerk giving notice that an action or proceeding, affecting the title to a property, is pending in the courts.

LTV (Loan-to-Value Ratio): Refers to the amount of money loaned on a property relative to its actual value. For example, a loan of $20,000 on a $40,000 house would be a 50% LTV ratio.

Marketable Title: A title that the court considers to be so free from defect that it will enforce its acceptance by a purchaser.

Mechanic's Lien: A claim made to secure the price of labor done upon and materials furnished for uncompensated improvement.

Moratorium: An emergency act by a legislative body to suspend the legal enforcement of contractual obligations.

Mortgage: An instrument in writing, duly executed and delivered, that creates a lien on real estate as security for the payment of a specified debt, which is usually in the form of a bond.

Mortgage Broker: One who is paid to match borrowers with lenders.

Mortgagee: The party who lends money and takes a mortgage to secure their payment.

Mortgagor: A person who borrows money and gives a mortgage on his or her property as security for the payment of the debt.

Multiple Listing: An arrangement among members of the Board of REALTORS® whereby brokers bring their listings to the attention of the other members. If a sale results, the commission is divided between the broker providing the listing and the broker making the sale.

Non-Qualifying Assumption: A mortgage or deed of trust that does not contain a due-on-sale clause, thereby allowing transfer of title freely without permission from the lender.

Obsolescence: Loss in value due to reduced desirability and usefulness of a structure because its design and construction has become obsolete.

Open Listing: A listing given to any number of brokers with commissions payable only to the broker who secures the sale.

Open Mortgage: A mortgage that has matured or is overdue and, therefore, is "open" to foreclosure at any time.

Option: A right given for a consideration to purchase or lease a property upon specific terms within a specified time. If the right is not exercised, the option holder is not subject to liability for damages. If exercised, the grantor of option must perform.

Pay-off Letter: A letter from a lender stating the current balance due on an account; also referred to as an estoppel letter or certificate.

Performance Bond: A bond used to guarantee the specific completion of an endeavor in accordance with a contract.

Personal Property: Any property which is not real property.

Plat Book: A public record containing maps of land showing the division into streets, blocks, and lots and indicating the measurements of the individual parcels.

Points: Discount charges imposed by lenders to raise the yields on their loans. One (1) point equals one (1%) percent of the loan amount.

Prepayment Clause: A clause in a mortgage that gives a mortgagor the privilege of paying the mortgage indebtedness before it becomes due, either with or without prepayment penalty.

Proration: Allocation of closing costs and credits to buyers and sellers.

Purchase Money Mortgage: A mortgage given by a grantee or any other lender in partial payment of the purchase price of real estate.

Quiet Title Suit: A suit in court to ascertain the legal rights of an owner to a certain parcel of real property.

Quitclaim Deed: A deed that conveys simply the grantor's rights or interest, if any, in real estate; generally considered inadequate except when interests are being passed from one spouse to the other.

Real Estate Board: An organization whose members consist primarily of real estate brokers and salespersons.

REO (Real Estate Owned): Property acquired by a lender through foreclosure and held in inventory.

Real Estate Syndicate: A partnership formed for a real estate venture. Partners may be limited or unlimited in their liability.

Real Property: Land and generally whatever is erected upon or affixed thereto.

REALTOR®: A term used to identify active members of the National Association of REALTORS® (NAR®), This term is commonly used to refer to anyone licensed to sell real estate. However, the term "REALTOR®" only applies to those dues-paying members of NAR.

Recording: The act of writing or entering, in a book of public record, instruments affecting the title to real property.

Recourse: The right to claim against an owner of a property or note.

Red Lining: The refusal to lend money within a specific area for various reasons. This practice is illegal because it discriminates against creditworthy people who happen to live there.

Release Clause: A clause found in a blanket mortgage which gives the owner of the property the privilege to pay off part of the debt, and thus free part of the property from the mortgage.

Repo: A shortened or slang version of repossession.

Repossession: Repossession occurs when a lender takes possession of the collateral which was security for a loan.

Right of Redemption: Right to recover property transferred by a mortgage or other lien by paying off the debt either before or after foreclosure; also called equity of redemption.

Right of Survivorship: Right of the surviving joint owner to succeed to the interests of the deceased joint owner. This right is a distinguishing feature of a joint tenancy or tenancy by the entirety.

RTC (Resolution Trust Corporation): An organization set up by the government to market houses from the inventory of federally insured, defunct banks and other lending institutions.

Sales Contract: A contract by which the buyer and seller agree to terms of sale.

Second Mortgage: A mortgage made by a home buyer in addition to an existing first mortgage. The order of recording determines the seniority of the lien.

Seller Financing: Refers to the owner of a property who agrees to carry a mortgage on the property that he or she is selling, so that the buyer doesn't have to obtain any or all of the financing from another source or lending institution.

Specific Performance: A remedy in a court of equity compelling a defendant to carry out the terms of an agreement or contract.

Split Funding: A technique whereby an investor offers a small amount of cash to close the deal with the balance due at a later date in a form other than extended monthly payments.

Statute of Frauds: Law requiring certain contracts to be made in writing or partially complied with in order to be legally enforceable.

Subdivision: A tract of land divided into lots or plots.

Subordination: See Subordination Clause.

Subordination Clause: A clause in a mortgage that gives priority to a mortgage taken out at a later date. The seller agrees to go into a second, third or fourth position allowing you to obtain new financing senior to their lien without paying them off from the proceeds.

Substitution of Collateral: Taking an existing mortgage on one property and transferring it to another.

Survey: The process by which a parcel of land is measured and its area ascertained; also the blueprint showing the measurements, boundaries, and area.

Tax Sale: Sale of real property after a period of non-payment of real estate taxes.

Tenancy in Common: An ownership of realty by two or more persons, each of whom has an undivided interest, without the right of survivorship.

Tenancy by the Entirety: An estate that exists only between husband and wife with equal right of possession and enjoyment during their joint lives and with the right of survivorship.

Tenancy at Will: A license to use or occupy lands and tenements at the will of the owner.

Testate: Condition when a person dies leaving a valid will.

TPA (Third Party Administrator): One who is approved to administer funds from a retirement program. You must use a TPA to access money from your retirement accounts for self-directed activities.

Title Company: A firm that examines title to real estate and/or issues title insurance.

Title Insurance: An insurance policy usually issued at the time of closing insuring against any title defects which could render the title unmarketable.

Title Report: A document indicating the current state of the title, such as easements, covenants, liens, and any other defects. The title report may not describe the chain of title.

Title Search: An examination of the public records to determine the ownership and encumbrances affecting real property.

Transfer Tax: A tax charged on the property upon transfer of title.

Trust Deed: Conveyance of real estate to a third party to be held for the benefit of another. It is commonly used in some states in place of mortgages that conditionally convey title to the lender.

Trustee: 1. One who holds legal title to property in trust for the benefit of another person, and who is required to carry out specific duties with regard to the property, or who has been given power affecting the disposition of property for another's benefit. 2. Loosely, anyone who acts as a guardian or fiduciary in relationship to another, such as a public officer toward his constituents, a state toward its citizens, or a partner to his co-partner.

Trustor: One who creates a trust, often called the settlor.

Undivided Interest: Ownership of real estate by joint tenants or tenants in common under the same title.

Usury: The lending of money at a rate of interest greater than that permitted by law.

VA: Veterans Administration; see VA Loan.

VA Loan: Mortgage loan insured by the Veterans Administration.

Variance: The authorization to improve or develop a particular property in a manner not authorized by zoning.

Warranty Deed: A conveyance of land in which the grantor guarantees the title to the grantee.

Without Recourse: Words used in endorsing a note or bill to denote that the future holder is not to look to the endorser in case of nonpayment.

Wrap (Wraparound Loan): A new loan encompassing any existing loans.

APPENDICES

A.   Property Acquisition Worksheet

B.   Bird Dog Flyer

C.   Property Information Sheet

D.   Letter to an Out-of-State Owner

E.   Subordination Agreement

F.   Notice of Substitution of Collateral

G.   Telephone Questionnaire for Potential Buyers

H.   Getting Your House Ready to Market

I.   Authorization to Release Information

J.   Causes and Cures of Failure

APPENDIX A

Property Acquisition Worksheet

Address:_____

1. Sale price after fix-up   _____
2. Down payment   _____
3. Purchase closing costs   _____
4. Commission   _____
5. Appraisal   _____
6. Termite   _____
7. Survey   _____
8. Misc.   _____
9. Total acquisition expense   (-)_____
10. Repair budget   _____
11. Cost overruns   _____
12. Total fix-up costs   (-)_____
13. Payments for six months   _____
14. Property tax   _____
15. Insurance   _____
16. Utilities   _____
17. Total holding costs   (-)_____
18. Sale closing costs   _____
19. Commission   _____
20. Advertising   _____
21. Total sale costs   (-)_____

Sale price less lines 9, 12, 17, 21 $_____

Mortgage payoffs   (-)_____

ESTIMATED NET PROFIT $_____

CASH REQUIREMENT
(Lines 9,12,13,15,16,20) $_____

APPENDIX B
BIRD DOG

Make $2,000 A Month

NO CREDIT — NO MONEY — VERY LITTLE KNOWLEDGE

- Write down the phone numbers on all For Sale By Owner (FSBO) signs, then call those numbers and get information sheets completed.

- Fill out information sheets on any and all houses for sale by private owners. Do this for FSBOs and any other houses you can find.

- Submit those sheets to my office.

YOU GET $250 IF WE BUY

- Make up an information sheet on all vacant houses not listed with REALTORS®, especially if the houses are run down.

- Try to locate owner's name, address, and phone number.

- Submit sheets to my office.

For Bird Doggers!

YOU GET $250 if we buy and you furnished owner's information.

YOU GET $100 if we buy and you did not furnish owner's information.

APPENDIX C

Property Information Sheet

Submitted by:_____

Date:_____ Phone:_____

Address:_____

Area:_____

This is a FSBO:_____Listed:_____

Other:_____

Owner's name:_____Owner's Phone:_____

Owner's address:_____

_____

Asking price: $_____

Terms:_____

Existing mortgages:

1st

$_____Lender_____Rate____Pmt____FHA/VA/Conv____

2nd

$_____Lender_____Rate____Pmt____FHA/VA/Conv____

Does house need repairs?_____ General description of repairs: _____

_____

Bedrooms_____Baths_____ Construction_____

Central Heat_____ Central Air_____

Garage_____Range_____ Refr_____

Is the house: Vacant_____Occupied_____

EXTRAS: _____

_____

COMMENTS:_____

_____

APPENDIX D

Letter To an Out-Of-State Owner

YOUR NAME.
Address
City, State, ZIP

Dear Homeowner:

We are a group of investors who buy and sell houses in the Jacksonville area. Through public records, we are aware of the property you own here in Jacksonville. If you are interested in selling and need FAST CASH, please call Bob at ( ) -   or, if you prefer, you can fill out the bottom portion of this letter and mail it to us at the address above. We guarantee you an offer, and we will be in contact with you as soon as we receive the information listed at the bottom.

We are looking forward to doing business with you, and have a GREAT NEW YEAR !

Sincerely,

Your Name

_____ YES, I am interested in selling my property located at

_____

I am asking $_____ for the property.
It is ( ) Occupied ( ) Vacant.
NAME:_____
ADDRESS:_____
CITY:_____ STATE:_____ ZIP: _____
PHONE #: _____
NOTES:_____
_____
_____
_____

We will inspect the property from the exterior and call you shortly with an offer.

APPENDIX E

Subordination Agreement

THIS SUBORDINATION AGREEMENT MADE this _____
day of_____, 19_, by and between _____,
mortgagor and_____, mortgagee.

WITNESSETH:

WHEREAS, the mortgagees are the owners and holders of
that certain mortgage executed by mortgagor and recorded on
_____, in Official Records, Vol____, Page_____, of the
current public records of _____
County_____City_____ State_____,
which secures that certain mortgage note in the original principal sum of _____(the "mortgage"),
and

WHEREAS, the mortgagor intends to refinance the property
secured by said note and requires this Subordination of
Mortgage as a condition precedent to purchasing said property.

NOW, THEREFORE, in consideration of the promises and of
the advantages to be derived from the execution and delivery of
this agreement, the mortgagee further agrees that the mortgagor shall automatically be entitled to refinance any currently
existing, prior, or new liens and/or mortgages encumbering the
subject real property, and upon the recordation of any mortgages or liens that act as the refinancing of said prior or new
mortgages, same shall automatically be considered superior to
the lien of the mortgage, no matter when same shall have been
recorded. This agreement is intended to operate as an automatic subordination agreement whereby the mortgagee agrees and
has agreed to subordinate the lien of their mortgage to the refinancing of any prior liens and/or new mortgages without the
necessity of recording an additional subordination agreement.

FURTHER, mortgagees represent and warrant that they are the sole owners of said mortgage and have full power and authority to execute and deliver this Subordination Agreement.

IN WITNESS WHEREOF, the parties have caused this instrument to be executed and their seals affixed the day and year first above written.

_____   _____
Witness   Seal

_____   _____
Witness   Seal

_____   _____
Witness   Seal

STATE OF_____

COUNTY OF_____

On _____, 199___, before me, a Notary Public, personally appeared _____ , _____ and _____ , known to me (or proven to me) to be the persons set forth above who acknowledged that they had executed the foregoing document for the purposes contained therin. Witness my hand and official seal.

_____

NOTARY PUBLIC STATE OF_____

MY COMMISSION EXPIRES_____

Notice of Substitution
of Collateral

The undersigned herewith files this "Notice of Substitution of Collateral" notifying all interested persons and parties that from this date forward the mortgage dated the _____ day of_____, 19____, and recorded under Clerk's number_____, of the public records of _____County, _____, is herewith modified and amended to substitute for the collateral therein described as the security for said mortgage to the real property more particularly described as:

Hereinafter, the real property currently described in said mortgage and note are forever released from the lien of this mortgage, and the lien of same is herewith transferred to the real property described herein above.

This notice is filed pursuant to the terms of that certain "Agreement for Substitution of Collateral" previously filed herein and recorded under Clerk's number_____, of the public records of _____ County, _____.

IN WITNESS WHEREOF, I have set my hand and official seal on the_____day of _____, 19_____.

Signed and sealed in our presence as witnesses:

_____   _____

_____   _____

STATE OF_____

COUNTY OF_____

BEFORE ME personally appeared_____to me well known and known to me to be the individual described in and who executed the foregoing instrument, and acknowledged to and before me that he executed the same for the purposes therein expressed.

WITNESS my hand and official seal this _____day of_____, 19___, at_____County and State aforesaid.

_____
NOTARY PUBLIC, STATE AND COUNTY
AFORESAID

My commission expires:

APPENDIX G

Telephone Questionnaire for Potential Buyers

Date:_____ Source of call: _____

Name:_____

Address:_____

City:_____State:_____ ZIP:_____

Phone: W _____ H _____

What is the maximum down payment available?_____

What price range?_____

Maximum payment affordable?_____

What areas are acceptable?_____

How many bedrooms and bathrooms required?_____

Construction preferred?___Frame ___Brick ___Concrete block

Is a garage mandatory?_____

How is credit?____Good ____Fair ____ Poor

When are you ready to buy?_____

What is the problem (If there is one)?_____

_____

How many square feet are needed? _____

Other requirements:_____

_____

_____

_____

_____

_____

Comments:_____

_____

_____

_____

_____

_____

APPENDIX H

Getting Your House Ready to Market

A checklist of suggestions for fixing up your property

EXTERIOR
Fix up front first
Landscape, clean yard, trim trees and shrubs, edge driveway
Paint using semi-gloss, two colors
Hang shutters
Hang large house numbers
Install fancy front door
Put in new windows if needed, at least in front

KITCHEN
Replace cabinet fronts
Install nice-looking sink, new knobs
Hang wallpaper with borders
Lay shiny new linoleum floor
Hang up a deodorizer (cinnamon spice)
Appliances not mandatory
Install fancy wall plugs
Install ceiling fan
Put up mini-blinds
Install smoke alarm

LIVING ROOM
Add some bright paneling
Add molding at ceiling
Hang inexpensive curtains or mini blinds
Lay carpet and pad (have a professional do the work)
Install ceiling fans

BATHROOMS
Refinish tub and sink if necessary

Put marolite over bad walls

Hang wallpaper with border

Replace ugly faucets

Hang shower curtain

Install mini-blinds

Use denture tablets to clean toilets

BEDROOMS

Paint with semi-gloss, trim in different shade

Do not strip wood and restain

Consider cedar in closet

Install ceiling fan

Wallpaper at least part of master bedroom

Install mini-blinds

Lay carpet and pad